ZAMP KELP

Torsten Schmiedeknecht

ZAMP KELP
EXPANDING SPACE

Architectural Monographs 54

WILEY-ACADEMY

In February 1998 I first met Zamp Kelp in his office in Düsseldorf to conduct an interview with him for *Architectural Design*. It was a meeting that I had long anticipated. When I met Zamp Kelp I was very pleasantly surprised by his modesty and his willingness to cooperate. The person I met was a very friendly, humorous and entertaining character. This first impression has been deepened during the period that we have been working on this book and I would like to take the opportunity to thank Zamp Kelp and to wish him all the best.

Furthermore, my thanks are to the late Prof. David Thistlewood of the University of Liverpool who has inspired this project and to Prof. Simon Pepper of the same institution who helped with the editing of Zamp Kelp's texts. Thanks also to Prof. David Dunster for his support. I would also like to thank my two conversation partners Steven Spier, recently appointed Professor at the School of Architecture, Strathclyde University in Glasgow, and Paul Davies from South Bank University in London for their cooperation, patience and help. Thanks to the layout consultants Jürgen Wolf & Cie. and to Frank O'Sullivan of Kingston University for helpful advice. Thanks to Justin DeSyllas and Avanti Architects in London for their patience and cooperation. Thanks to everyone at Wiley Academy and Artmedia. Special thanks to my parents for their love and support. And last but not least thanks to my wife Julia for her love, support and never ending enthusiasm about the project.

Torsten Schmiedeknecht

Cover and Frontispiece: *Millennium View – Model*

First published in Great Britain in 2000 by
WILEY–ACADEMY

A division of
JOHN WILEY & SONS
Baffins Lane
Chichester
West Sussex PO19 1UD

ISBN: 0-471-85404-2

Other Wiley Editorial Offices
New York • Weinheim • Brisbane • Singapore • Toronto

Designed by Artmedia, London

Printed and bound in Italy

Contents

Surface, Metaphor and Virtuality
Torsten Schmiedeknecht

> *Modernity is the transient, the fleeting, the contingent; it is the one half of art, the other being the eternal and the immutable.*[1]
>
> Charles Baudelaire

In order to understand Zamp Kelp's recent work, it is necessary to trace the beginning of his architectural career when he co-founded and worked with the Austrian group of architects and artists Haus-Rucker-Co;[2] here, two essays by Stanislaus von Moos[3] and Dieter Bogner[4] provide invaluable starting points. It is also important to understand the broader architectural context of Austria and Vienna in the fifties and sixties; tracing the development of the architectural avantgarde during this period affords a chance to evaluate the meaning of Modernism and Postmodernism in Zamp Kelp's work. It also sets the scene for an exploration of the theme of 'expanding space' in his recent work, and an examination of the strategies and tactics he uses in order to translate his intellectual concepts into buildings.

Zamp Kelp in the Sixties

Haus-Rucker-Co and Vienna - Sixties and Seventies

If one had to name three catchwords as reminders of the web of imaginations that was crucial to the long-term development of Haus-Rucker-Co they would have to be: Buckminster Fuller, the Utopia of a non-individual but collective practise of art and Pop Art. [5]

In his essay 'Kunst und Technik: Direktkoppelungen' (Art and Technology: Direct Links) Stanislaus von Moos draws a line of influences and references from Russian Constructivism and Futurism via Dada and Surrealism, Pop Art, Alison and Peter Smithson and Archigram to Haus-Rucker-Co. Von Moos establishes these links by exploring various groups of projects and by illustrating both formal and intellectual similarities with the precedents. The fact that Von Moos' strategy is successful throws light on to the formal language of the architecture of Haus-Rucker-Co: it is non-specific and not linked to one formal approach, making it appropriate to classify the group's style(s) as non-modernist. However, as Von Moos points out, Haus-Rucker-Co carried through at least two themes that can be classified as being in the spirit of modernism: firstly, it regarded technology as a positive challenge presenting opportunities and, secondly, the group had a profound belief in abolishing the gap between art and life.

Jonathan Raban's book *Soft City* has been described as presenting one of the first post-modern descriptions of the city:

Signals, styles, systems of rapid, highly conventionalised communication, are the lifeblood of every city ... The city, our great modern form, is soft, amenable to the dazzling and libidinous variety of lives, dreams, interpretations. But the very plastic qualities which make the great city the liberator of human identity also cause it to be especially vulnerable to psychosis and totalitarian nightmare.[6]

If we leave Baudelaire's definition of modernity unchallenged and simultaneously look at Raban's view of the city, it is appropriate to locate both Haus-Rucker-Co and Zamp Kelp's work within the meaning of both quotations. The work carries strong characteristics of early modern thinking [7] and in practice it belongs also to the era of postmodernity.[8]

Günter (later Zamp) Kelp was born in 1941 in Bistritz, Romania, the youngest of three children. His father, a civil engineer, originally intended his youngest son to follow in his footsteps. At the age of three Günter Kelp and his family moved to Linz/Donau in Austria where he grew up, before moving to Vienna in 1959 to take up his study of architecture at the Technische Universität.

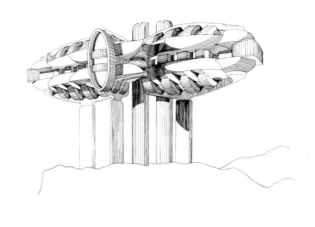

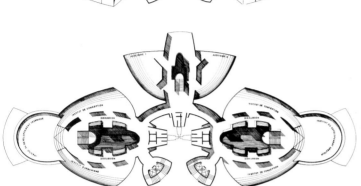

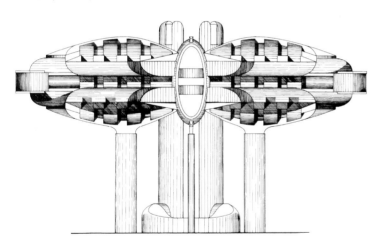

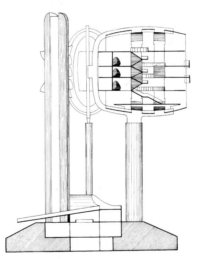

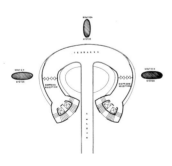

Zamp Kelp: Architekturtrainer 1965

The intellectual climate in Vienna in the early sixties was determined by the work of people like Hans Hollein, Walter Pichler, Hermann Nitsch, Peter Handke and Hermann Czech.[9]

According to Zamp Kelp's own accounts, the first years of his architecture course were neither particularly enjoyable nor successful. In 1963, however, there were changes at the Technische Universität that had a major impact on his development. Karl Schwanzer, architect of the Museum des 20.Jahrhunderts in Vienna, became a professor of design and building studies at the school and appointed Günter Feuerstein as his assistant. Schwanzer and Feuerstein encouraged the students to explore their creative potential in a new way. Feuerstein inaugurated the so-called Club-Seminar that took place once a week at the Galerie nächst Sankt Stephan, which soon became an important forum for the exchange of information and opinion outside the university. Amongst other activities, a field trip to the USA was organised and the students were able to meet Philip Johnson, John Johansen, Frederic Kiesler, Louis Kahn and Paul Rudolph, and thus in discussions to become familiar with the personalities behind the architectural work that they had already known. The trip to the USA was stimulating and for most of the participants it was their first time out of Europe or even Austria.

This new inspiration was reflected in the students' work. Zamp Kelp's first recorded architectural work is his student project 'Architekturtrainer' from 1965, described in his text 'Vom Monument Zum Ereignis' (From Monument to Event): *The project 'Architecture Trainer' stands diametrically opposed to Boullée's monuments.[10] In reverie it floats on five verticals over the top of the Spatzenberg near Linz. In different climatic moods, a Puzzle Picture from the outside, it shifts between reality and projection in the eyes of the viewer. A school of architecture on the inside, it also serves as a platform for the observation of urban landscape. Being a permanent 'mirage' on the horizon of the city, the aura of its external appearance lends the character of event to the project.[11]*

Even though the above quotation is taken from a text written almost thirty years after the project had been drawn, it illustrates Zamp Kelp's early interest in the phenomenon of projection. Projection and the importance of our understanding of its relevance and impact on our perception of space have since become key factors in his writings and architectural work. The first project in which Zamp Kelp fully explored the possibilities of the means of projection for the generation of architectural space was his student project 'Architekturschleuder' (Architecture Sling) from 1966, in which images were projected on to rotating mirror blades that in turn threw the images on to the surrounding walls and ceilings of an interior space. The project was part of the exhibition 'Urban Fiction' organised by Günter Feuerstein at the Galerie nächst Sankt Stephan.[12]

After Zamp Kelp graduated in 1967, he became an assistant to professor Karl Schwanzer at the Institute for Design and Building Studies at the Technische Universität in Vienna. A competition called Interdesign 2000 was launched at the same time by the German firm Holzäpfel and provided the opportunity for Zamp Kelp and his contemporaries Helmut Grasberger, Manfred and Laurids Ortner, Edith Ortner, Herbert Schweiger, Angela Hareiter and Klaus Pinter to explore further their design solutions for an ever-changing environment. The competition's objective was to examine new and innovative concepts of living. The group split into two teams and entered the competition with the projects Mind Expander and Pneumacosm. Zamp Kelp's group project Pneumacosm was a Plug-In living cell that came as a unit and was supposed to work like a light bulb: the moment that it was plugged into its station all services like electricity, water and telecommunications would be provided.

Mind Expander was a seat for two people over which a helmet situated within a PVC balloon could be pulled. Both helmet and balloon had vivid patterns printed or stuck on to them and the users' experiences were determined by which one of the layers they focused on. As Laurids Ortner was to put it: *A small device transforms air into a building material. Architecture made from air. A technological comeback of the roots of all building. The new requirements*

Projection and the importance of our understanding of its relevance and impact on our perception of space have since become key factors in his writings and architectural work.

Zamp Kelp: Architekturschleuder 1966

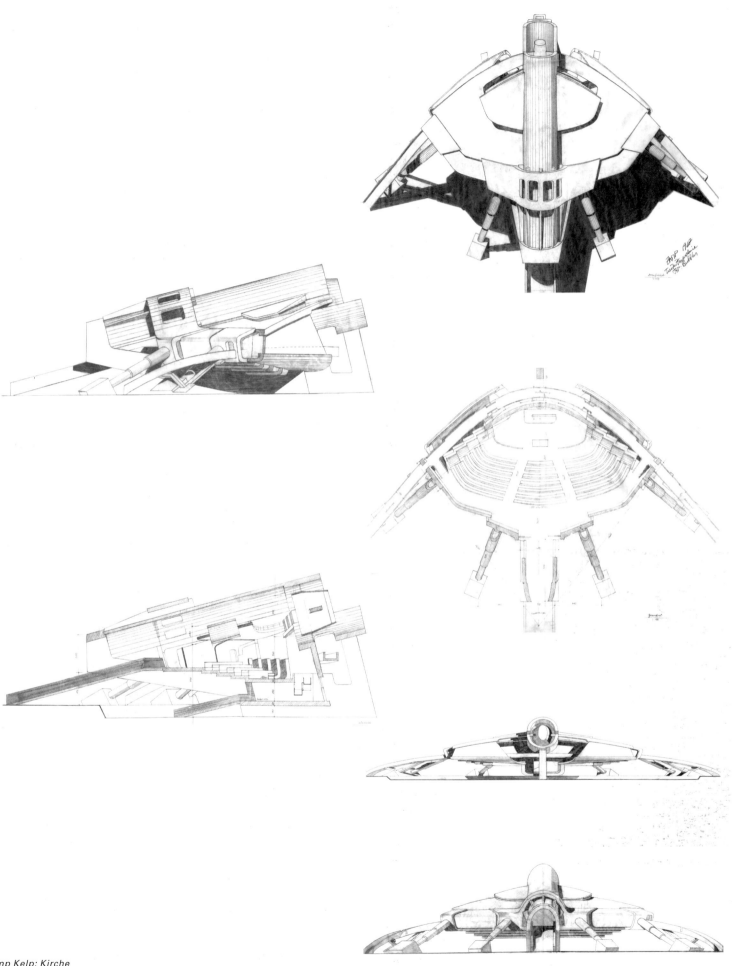

Zamp Kelp: Kirche

Haus-Rucker-Co: Mind Expander, Vienna, 1967

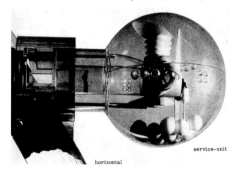

Haus-Rucker-Co: Pneumacosm, Vienna, 1967

Haus-Rucker-Co: Ballon Für Zwei, Vienna, 1967

for mobility and changeability can be fulfilled by soft and flexible forms of building. We can overcome the right angle just by the abilities and possibilities of the new materials. The transformation of society simply because it is moving within soft and flowing structures: on soft wings into another way of thinking.[13]

Dieter Bogner regards Pneumacosm and Mind Expander, despite being pre Haus-Rucker-Co, as the quasi founding manifesto of the group. He distinguishes between Pneumacosm as a proposal radically to rethink the notion of physical space, belonging into the realm of visionary and utopian architecture, and Mind Expander as a project within the realms of psychological space, addressing the issue of man's 'inner' space.

... one is an architectural proposal to create space for the body, the other is an artistic instrument to enter the space of one's consciousness.[14]

Influenced by Archigram[15] and encouraged by the recognition that Pneumacosm and Mind Expander had gained, Zamp Kelp together with Laurids Ortner and Klaus Pinter formed the group Haus-Rucker-Co in the Cafe Poechacker in Vienna in September 1967. Hausruck is the name of the area in Upper Austria where Kelp, Ortner and Pinter spent their childhood. Haus also means 'house' in German and Ruck derives from the German word *rücken* which means 'to move' or 'to shift'. The name Haus-Rucker-Co, therefore, not only alluded to the origins of the three members but also encapsulated a programme: 'to shift houses conceptually in our ideas and realisations'.[16] The afternoon in September 1967 was the beginning of a period when the group mainly tried to create a profile associated with the name Haus-Rucker-Co.

The quick result, the direct implementation of projects into reality through common efforts, was the most important element for the group in the beginning. This was what gave the group the feeling of a fruitful co-operation.[17]

The first commonly executed project by Haus-Rucker-Co was an installation called Ballon Für Zwei. In an interview conducted in February 1998, Zamp Kelp reflected:

... a forerunner [of virtual reality] was the Ballon Für Zwei ... It appeared six times between 12.00 am and 6.00 pm ... through a window of a Viennese ... facade. Each appearance lasted for about ten minutes, creating the opportunity for a male/female couple to experience the ... urban environment through the tattooed, transparent membrane of the spherical balloon. In Ballon Für Zwei ... the membrane was situated between the organ of visual perception (the eye) and the environment. This obstruction or hindrance was aimed at the relearning of perception.[18]

Ballon Für Zwei clearly expressed Zamp Kelp and Haus-Rucker-Co's interest in, and fascination with, the condition of human perception and its causal relationship with awareness and consciousness.[19]

These early projects have to be looked at in the context of the general mood among the architectural and artistic avant-garde in Vienna at the time. In 1962, Hans Hollein and Walter Pichler wrote their manifesto *Absolute Architecture* which was followed by their exhibition entitled 'Architektur. Work in Progress' at the Galerie nächst Sankt Stephan.

This architecture is not a matter of beauty. If we desire beauty at all, it is not so much beauty of form, of proportion, as a sensual beauty of elemental force ... A building ought not to display its utilitarian function, is not the expression of structure and construction, is not a covering or a refuge. A building is itself. Architecture is purposeless ... we build what and how we will, we make an architecture that is not determined by technology but utilises technology, a pure, absolute architecture. Today man is master over infinite space.[20]

Absolute Architecture marked the end of one of the three dominant schools of modernist thought in Vienna. Hollein and Pichler reintroduced the ideas of the myth, the ritual and the symbol into architectural thinking[21] and can be seen as the instigators of a line of thought that criticised existing circumstances, and advocated the idea of a total architecture that would eventually lead to the abolition of the idea itself.[22] Another contemporary attitude was a modernist movement that negated any dialogue or relationship with history and argued mainly functionalist and purist views. Roland Rainer's design for the Stadthalle Wien (1953-58) and Karl

The quick result, the direct implementation of projects into reality through common efforts, was the most important element for the group in the beginning. This was what gave the group the feeling of a fruitful co-operation.

Most art forms and concepts are inherently linked to the intention of changing the societies of which they are part. Haus-Rucker-Co's concept of society's awareness finds its first precedent in the ideas of Russian Constructivism and early modern utopian thoughts.

Schwanzer's Österreich Pavilion in Brussels (1958) are good examples of the inherently positivist belief in structure and construction. The third school of thought sought to establish a relationship with Vienna's own past within the twentieth century and started to re-acknowledge people like Wagner, Hoffmann and Loos who had been deliberately ignored in the years since the First World War, while at the same time studying the work of contemporaries like Egon Eiermann and Konrad Wachsmann. The most widely known group advocating this more open notion of architecture was the Arbeitsgruppe 4, consisting of Friedrich Kurrent, Wilhelm Holzbauer, Friedrich Achleitner and Johannes Spalt.[23]

The theory and practice of Haus-Rucker-Co consisted of elements of all three ideologies. With Pichler and Hollein it shared the urge to criticise and comment on current circumstances and to open up the architectural debate. Simultaneously, there appear strong positivist tendencies in the group's thinking that are related to the Enlightenment project in that it is pursuing very specific aims with specific means.[24] However, as Stanislaus von Moos has illustrated, there is also an awareness of historical developments inherent in Haus-Rucker-Co's work. Thus, Haus-Rucker-Co's work is above all inclusive. The merging of these different fragments of thought in its projects indicates Haus-Rucker-Co's role as one of the first groups of architects to operate within the realm of postmodernity.

One of the main objectives of Haus-Rucker-Co was to raise urban dwellers' awareness of their surroundings, which would in turn lead to changes in society that the group felt were necessary. In order to achieve this, a whole series of projects, summarised under the title Mind Expanding Programme, was executed.[25] Most art forms and concepts are inherently linked to the intention of changing the societies of which they are part. Haus-Rucker-Co's concept of society's awareness finds its first precedent in the ideas of Russian Constructivism and early modern utopian thought.[26] The urge to reveal the creative power of the masses and to overcome the distinction between the artist and the rest of society in Constructivism was highly politically motivated, since Constructivism was the first modern movement to be so strongly attached to an ideology. However, Haus-Rucker-Co's concepts were never linked to any particular political movement and they deliberately distanced themselves from the so-called 'Wiener Aktionismus' that arose from the student revolts of the late sixties. Haus-Rucker-Co's strongest link with Constructivist and early modern utopian ideas was realised in the group's belief that mass culture would eventually replace high art. Thus the projects of the Mind Expanding Programme and the later Temporary Architecture Series were mainly located in the urban environment in the form of installations that would enable urban dwellers to gain new physical and psychological experiences of their surroundings. Illustrating the importance of awareness of the individual in Haus-Rucker-Co's work, Stanislaus von Moos quotes another source of reference, the Situationniste Constant Nieuwenhuis.

The core of the cultural revolution in the 20th Century is turning the notion of creativity from a fixed individual expression towards a collective, experimental practice.[27]

Modern technology, innovation, metamorphosis and change, and contemporary mass media, as well as the supposedly trivial detail of everyday life and the condition of human perception in the city, appealed as fields of exploration that were to serve as the source of inspiration for Haus-Rucker-Co and Zamp Kelp's work respectively. In England, Alison and Peter Smithson in the mid fifties – and later Archigram – had already started to explore the so-called everyday and mass media, and their effects and potential for architectural activities. Two key exhibitions were held in London at this time in which the Smithsons participated: 'Parallel of Life and Art' at the ICA, in 1953, and 'This is Tomorrow' at the Whitechapel Gallery, in 1956. 'Parallel of Life and Art' investigated what would later be described by Marshall McLuhan as 'The Medium is the Message'. By exhibiting black and white photographs of objects from the most diverse scales, times and cultural backgrounds, any notion of traditional hierarchies between the exhibits was overcome. The exhibition was testing a medium and thus the viewers' perception of it. 'This is Tomorrow' was

At the same time that Haus-Rucker-Co acknowledged the influences that shaped its own work, the group itself started playing an important role internationally in terms of its influence on other experimental architects and groups.

Haus-Rucker-Co: Oase No.7, Kassel, 1972

a show in which twelve groups consisting of painters, sculptors and architects were each given a space to execute an installation. The project by the Smithsons, carried out in collaboration with the sculptor Eduardo Paolozzi and the photographer Nigel Henderson, was called Patio and Pavilion. It is of interest in the context of Haus-Rucker-Co's work because it pre-empts an element of Haus-Rucker-Co's project Oase No.7.[28] The Smithsons wrote that Patio and Pavilion *"represents the fundamental necessities of the human habitat in a series of symbols. The first necessity is for a piece of the world, the patio; the second necessity is for an enclosed space, the pavilion. These two spaces are furnished with symbols for all human needs"*.[29] Describing Oase No.7, Stanislaus von Moos states that in his view Haus-Rucker-Co's interest in the future was mainly to do with the primordial, with the beginnings, and in Oase No.7 Von Moos sees the primitive hut in the form of a space capsule. Zamp Kelp's pursuit of the identity of place in his contemporary work is clearly a continuation of these early observations. The difference between Haus-Rucker-Co's primitive hut, as Von Moos points out, and other concepts of the primitive hut – for example, Le Corbusier's tent, or Laugier's interpretation with columns and beams – is that it is non-monumental. This is not dissimilar to the Smithsons' interpretation.

Archigram had been clearly influenced by the Smithsons and their activities. As Hans Hollein put it, Archigram believed that architecture was a medium of communication – and the work of Haus-Rucker-Co is also deeply rooted in this belief – which led it to approach the activity of architecture from various different view points.

Architecture is only a small part of city environment in terms of real significance; the total environment is what is important, what really matters. The object ...[is] to determine the effect total environment has on the human condition, the response it generates – and to capture, to express, the vitality of the city. We must perpetuate this vitality or the city will die at the hands of the hard planners and architect-aesthetes.[30]

Apart from Archigram's writings, the imagery the group produced was an inspiration to the members of Haus-Rucker-Co. Zamp Kelp's Architekturtrainer and Kirche, or Laurids Ortner's 47.Stadt and Architekturschule are hard to imagine without the precedents of Archigram's Walking City, and Pneumacosm bears conceptual similarities to the Plug-In City. The difference between Archigram and Haus-Rucker-Co, though, is that the latter always regarded the city as a laboratory for its experiments. Putting an idea to the test by physically confronting the public with it was not part of Archigram's programme. Archigram's field of experiment was located in the media through which it distributed its ideas. Haus-Rucker-Co's members, despite their activities as writers, were always concerned with the actual making of the objects they had designed. This tradition has been carried on until today with Zamp Kelp and the brothers Laurids and Manfred Ortner still very much involved in architectural production and building. The development that had started in 1967 is still going on in the work of their individual practices.

At the same time that Haus-Rucker-Co acknowledged the influences that shaped its own work, the group itself started playing an important role internationally in terms of its influence on other experimental architects and groups. Archizoom and Natalini's Superstudio from Italy, as much as Archigram in London, closely observed the developments in Vienna and later Düsseldorf, and it is probably fair to say that ultimately the influence of Haus-Rucker-Co on the British scene was stronger than vice versa.

In *Denkräume-Stadträume (Think Space – City Space)*, Dieter Bogner describes the work of Haus-Rucker-Co as consisting of two main areas of interest – *Bewußtseinserweiterung* and *Stadtgestaltung* (expansion of consciousness/awareness and shaping of the city):
Where the first concern shaped the early years in the form of the Mind Expanding Programme, the second concern became more evident and gained importance in the theory and practice of the Provisorische Architektur (temporary, provisional architecture) from the mid seventies onwards.[31]

The fragmentation of space and the change in the relationship between subject and object that railway and film have caused are at the centre of Zamp Kelp's work.

According to Bogner, the interest in the expansion of consciousness/awareness led to a possible categorisation of areas of interest into utopian, psychological, public and ecological space; whereas shaping the city would mean considering 'city space', 'in-between space' and 'thinking space'. This analysis is useful when delineating groups of projects in Haus-Rucker-Co's work. Following on from Bogner's categorisation, one can establish the areas of interest in Zamp Kelp's work as a single practitioner. Thus the following table expresses the conceptual link between his work with Haus-Rucker-Co and as a single practitioner.

Bewußtseinserweiterung	
Haus-Rucker-Co	Zamp Kelp
psychological space	virtuality
utopian space	surface
public space	identity
ecological space	authenticity

Stadtgestaltung	
Haus-Rucker-Co	Zamp Kelp
city space	cultural landscape
in between space	perception
thinking space	translocation

Zamp Kelp has identified three groups of projects into which his work can be divided : identity, the representational and projection; observatories for culture, and additional elements. Within his projects, situated in the cultural landscape,[32] are rooted the key issues that he is concerned with: place / space / identity, programme, gesture / symbol / metaphor; perception / authenticity / translocation / virtuality and surface / texture.

Zamp Kelp in the Eighties

II Zamp Kelp – Eighties and Nineties

place / space / identity

... the image is interesting not only in its role as reflection, mirror, representation of ... the real, but also when it begins to contaminate reality and to model it, when it only conforms to reality the better to distort it, or better still: when it appropriates reality for its own ends, when it anticipates it to the point that the real no longer has time to be produced as such.[33]

Zamp Kelp's idea of expanding space is based on observations that he has made over the last thirty-five years, concerning the development of urban space and the way that it is perceived by the urban dweller. In his writings, he refers to the inventions that have taken place over the past two centuries and that have altered our perception of space and thus the way that space is being thought of and designed: the railway (acceleration, speed), film (television) and the Internet.[34]

The fragmentation of space and the change in the relationship between subject and object that railway and film have caused are at the centre of Zamp Kelp's work. Already in his work with Haus-Rucker-Co, the objective was to develop and invent devices in the form of temporary architectural installations to alter man's perception of the urban environment in order to adjust to the changed circumstances. In his current work, Zamp Kelp has maintained the objective, but the means with which he expresses his ideas have changed. He has now moved on to build buildings and thus the notion of the ephemeral in his work has shifted. Haus-Rucker-Co tried to cater for change with temporary constructions that would be very quick to build and to dismantle. Zamp Kelp, in his built work, has redefined his idea of the ephemeral. His buildings are specifically designed for a defined use of today. However, the ephemerality of any function or event is increasing in today's society and changes occur ever faster. Zamp Kelp's designs react to the phenomena of change by pursuing the creation of identity which is a means of protection and a

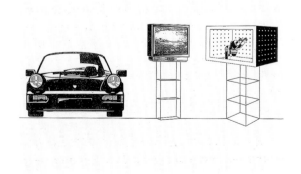

Zamp Kelp: Visual Machines, Nagoya, Japan, 1989

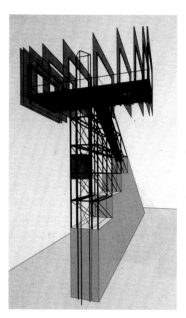

Zamp Kelp: Millennium View, Steinbergen, 1997-2000

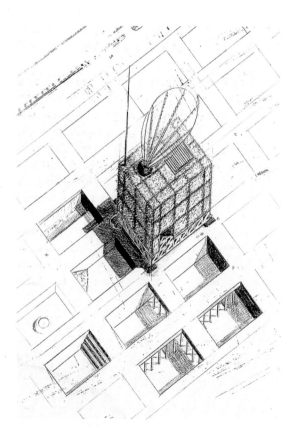

Zamp Kelp: Mekka Medial, Paris, 1990

question of survival in an environment that consists of images of all kinds of origins and media. How to create and sustain these identities is one of his key concerns. In his writings, Zamp Kelp mainly explores the possibilities that the mediated experience, resulting from projections, can offer.

Baudrillard's idea of the simulacrum and the obsolete reference principle between object and image offers one way of looking at the contemporary environment.[35] Architects such as Jean Nouvel counteract this notion with the idea of the intensification of the existing as opposed to the simulation of it. Zamp Kelp's position is similar to that of Nouvel. There are various spatial means that he employs in his projects to intensify the existing circumstances. The creation of height and views is a means that Zamp Kelp employs in most of his projects for public institutions. He guides visitors to a height from which they can locate themselves within the context, often providing long-distance views. The opposite effect is achieved when he digs out large quantities of the site in order to establish a physical relationship with it. The idea of the cut, for example – the revealing of the hidden, both metaphorically (history) and practically (matter) – is used in order to help people identify with the place and focus on it. Here, the question of territory becomes central. Territory in these respects must be looked at in different scales. The urban territory, or site, defining how the building locates itself in its environment, both physically and, on a larger scale, strategically within the city or landscape. The second notion of territory defines the hierarchy of spaces within the building and their individual relationships between each other and with the urban territory.

Within his work, Zamp Kelp identifies the problematic relationship between simulacrum and territory. The concept of the simulacrum denies the physical nature of place and object, and refers to the image as the means through which we perceive the world. The image is the world.

Reality is a key notion, but it is also problematic. It is one of Zamp Kelp's objectives to explore the nature of our perceived reality. The fact that the realm of our physical reality is constantly overlaid with images and impressions, and is thus being perceived as an amalgamation of both physical and virtual elements, presents a challenge to him rather than a problem. If we presume that any experience, however multilayered it might be is authentic (as opposed to Baudrillard's assumption), then any place and space can equally be so. What distinguishes Zamp Kelp's concept of authenticity from that of other contemporary architects is that he is willing to accept the world as it is. What he is concerned with is the way that we perceive it. The acceptance of the mediated experience as an authentic one allows him to include media of any kind to create space and thus place.

In his Mekka Medial project for Paris (1990), for example, the territory is physically strongly defined by the forty spaces, but the mobile cube, housing the broadcasting studio, extends the realm of this territory. Mediation is used consciously as a strategic design tool. An extended reality emerges that can be captured by the user because of the combination of physical and projected space. Thus the physical space gains a new importance as the stage for projections.

programme

Literate man, once having accepted an analytic technology of fragmentation, is not nearly so accessible to cosmic patterns as tribal man. He prefers separateness and compartmentalised spaces, rather than the open cosmos.[36]

Zamp Kelp's understanding of programme is based on the premise that architecture has to have more than three dimensions if it is to fulfil the needs of an ever-more complex world. In his view, architecture, as understood in the traditional sense, has lost its task and ability to shape society; this role has been taken over by the media. The contents of the media and communication networks, namely information, is in a constant state of flux. Zamp Kelp argues that architecture has to react to this if it is to regain a role beyond the simple production of built mass. Thus our understanding of space needs to be questioned. The meaning and appropriateness of spatial order have shifted in the twentieth century, and instead notions of dynamics and identity are to be considered. The programme of a building thus

The contents of the media and communication networks, namely information, is in a constant state of flux. Zamp Kelp argues that architecture has to react to this if it is to regain a role beyond the simple production of built mass.

goes beyond the simple adding up of square meters and rooms. Zamp Kelp sees the programme as being a social responsibility for the architect. His projects are always the result of a specific way of interpreting the programme. This interpretation contains, apart from the obvious resolution of functional problems, a socio-cultural concern with the task and circumstances at hand. Thus the interpretation of the programme not only determines spatial and functional constellations but also affects the role that the building, its client and its users will assume in their environment.

At first glance, this meticulous way of almost scientifically trying to resolve a specific programme in a specific situation seems to contradict Zamp Kelp's awareness of the need to react to change. It is a contradiction indeed, but not an unconscious one. Zamp Kelp is building for the moment, for today, since in his belief tomorrow will take care of itself. The future is unpredictable and thus the only buildings that will sustain meaning are the ones that are designed to answer today's needs. His projects, despite being designed so specifically, cater for changes in that they are strong enough to adapt to different circumstances. They might even have an impact on the changes that are being allowed to occur, since what we are doing today will shape our tomorrow.

When building, Zamp Kelp takes control of the project from an early stage, guiding the client through a thought process. This raises the question of the role of the architect, both as a professional in terms of dealing with clients, but also as an image. Zamp Kelp is the interpreter, the translator. He believes that the role of architects is to make society aware of certain issues through their specific skills, so that in turn society will change. This idea of a common awareness and consciousness which, if raised, would change society dates back to his early work with Haus-Rucker-Co.

In Zamp Kelp's work and his interpretation of programme, the idea of the matrix and the monument – if we replace monument with object building – becomes apparent. However, since in his view space in our time has lost its claim for finality, the object building or monument has to be reinterpreted. For Adolf Loos, the only forms of architecture belonging to art were the tomb and the monument.

The work of art is revolutionary, the house is conservative ... The work of art aims at shattering man's comfortable complacency ... Does the house therefore have nothing to do with art and should architecture not be classified as an art? This is so. Only a very small part of architecture belongs to art: the tomb and the monument.[37]

Tomb and Monument

For Zamp Kelp, the monument has become event, or rather, is being perceived as such. Thus architecture is being perceived as event.

For Zamp Kelp, the monument has become event, or rather, is being perceived as such. Thus architecture is being perceived as event. Zamp Kelp's attitude towards the programme and the event is somehow related, though not stylistically, to the way that Aldo Rossi illustrates the change of use of the Renaissance *palazzo*. Rossi tries to come to terms with the need for buildings to adapt to changing functions by using archetypal and recognisable typologies, aiming to create a spatial and social order. As Dan Graham noted in *Rock My Religion*, Rossi 'wishes to restore the archetypal, essential forms of the historical city and thereby restore collective memory.'[38]

Zamp Kelp does not employ archetypes, but his use of metaphor to create identity that goes beyond a limited period of time has the same objective. As opposed to Rossi, Zamp Kelp draws his concepts and interpretations from any cultural realm that seems suitable for a specific situation; he does not rely on any one architectural language or typology to illustrate his point of view.

gesture / symbol / metaphor

metaphor, a figure of speech in which a word or phrase is applied to an object or action that it does not literally denote in order to imply a resemblance, for example: he is a lion in battle. [39]

symbol, something that represents or stands for something else, usually by convention or association, esp. a material object used to represent something abstract. [40]

gesture, a motion of the hands, head or body to emphasise an idea or emotion, esp. when speaking. [41]

Metaphor, symbol and gesture are strong elements in Zamp Kelp's work, varying from the direct application of a gesture, the use of logos and imagery, to the total abstraction of a myth. The work shifts between Venturi's duck, the decorated shed and a modernist application of the metaphor.

The question of inside and outside in the context of the metaphor is an interesting one. Zamp Kelp's buildings visually work on different levels and the sum of the addressed issues provides the whole, the image. His buildings, both from the outside and from the inside, have an emotional and physical effect on people. Often one does not even have to be aware of what is going on intellectually: when arriving at the Neanderthal Museum in Mettmann (1993) for example, one instantly realises that something is different, that the place is special. The facade does not necessarily reveal what the building's function is, but because multiple aspects are addressed in the design – most of all in the design of the programme – and are carefully put together, the metaphor starts to work and the image of the building can be felt as a whole.

Gesture, symbol and metaphor provide an interesting opportunity to look at Zamp Kelp's work within the shift and the overlap of modernism and postmodernism.

Zamp Kelp: Museum Lanzarote, competition 1999

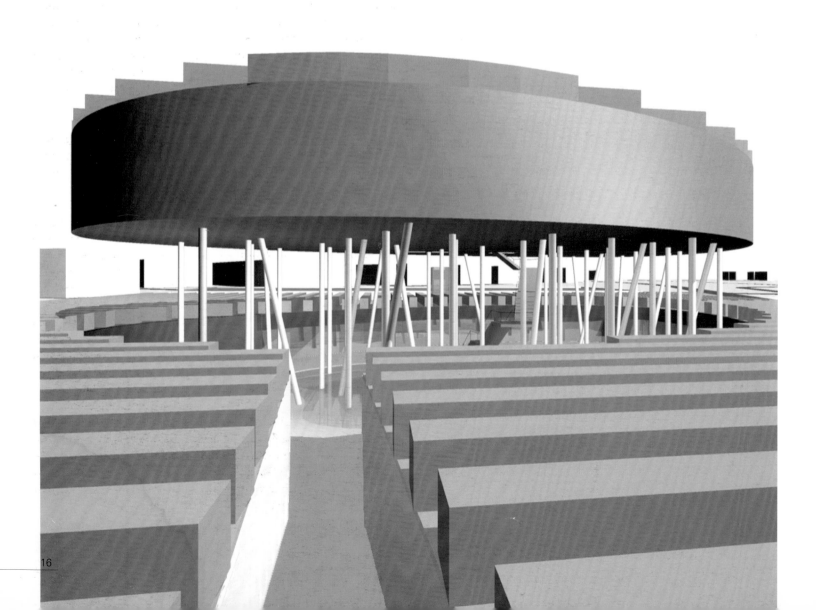

Zamp Kelp and J.Krauss / A.Brandlhuber:
Neanderthal Museum,
1994-96 Facade under construction

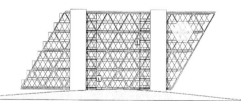

Zamp Kelp: *Fiege Headquarters,*
Airport Münster / Osnabruck,
competition 1997

The abstraction in both projects is derived from the modernist tradition, whereas the importance of the sustained identity of a specific place is a postmodern notion.

Modernism, employing abstraction as a means of expression, was in denial of the gesture, the direct application of the everyday story or object as a sign.[42] At the same time, modernism and early modern utopian thinking were rooted in the idea of the metanarrative, dating back to the Enlightenment project and the pursuit of reason. If we presume that postmodernism, in its reaction to modernism, is about plurality and the denial of the metanarrative but at the same time about the identity of place, Zamp Kelp's work seems to consist of a combination of elements of both modern and postmodern thinking. His use of the metaphor in the conceptual stage of a project, as a means to illustrate a specific identity for place and building, indicates a belief in the narrative. His idea of the narrative is closely related to that of modernism. At the same time, he employs different strategies to achieve his aim to build architecture as a means to aid a a better understanding of the world. As opposed to architects like Aldo Rossi or Oswald Mathias Ungers who (at the same time as Haus-Rucker-Co) reacted to modernism by adopting certain languages and typologies, Zamp Kelp's interpretations of metaphor, symbol and gesture are varied. For him, being a pluralist means constant reassessment, especially in terms of architectural language. Heinrich Klotz in *Die Revision Der Moderne* makes an interesting distinction between the postmodernism of Venturi on the one hand and of Rossi and Ungers on the other.[43] According to Klotz, Ungers and Rossi employ geometry and typology as their main strategic means. Like Zamp Kelp, they view content instead of function as the key for the development of programme.

The use of metaphor, symbol and gesture in Zamp Kelp's work has to be seen in the context of his views on the object / image relationship and the related tactics of intensification. The projects for the Millennium View in Steinbergen (1997-2000) and the Neanderthal Museum in Mettmann employ two strategies to re-establish the importance of the physical place and its identity. Firstly, both projects are developed through the use of the metaphor – the Millennium View and the surrounding park play with the idea of the journey of the quarry rock becoming building material, ending in a gravel pit; the Neanderthal Museum takes both the history of mankind and the history of the Neander Valley as starting points. Secondly, both projects become signs for the metaphor. Zamp Kelp argues that only that which develops identity will be able to sustain importance. Thus, these signs have to be able to survive both in the physical realm and in the realm of the media. Again ideas of modernism and postmodernism shift into each other: the abstraction in both projects is derived from the modernist tradition, whereas the importance of the sustained identity of a specific place is a postmodern notion.

Visual perception, the problem of authenticity and the phenomenon of translocation are strongly interlinked. According to Zamp Kelp, the phenomenon of translocation consists of 'the trinity of place, event and the transport of media'.

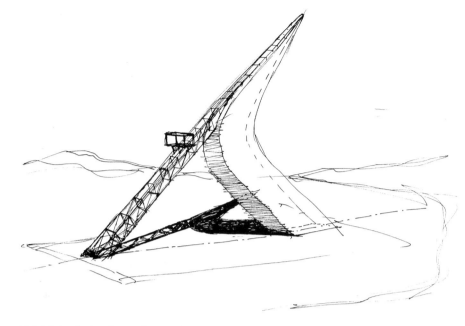

Zamp Kelp: Broken Lance, Lanzarote, competition 1999

Zamp Kelp: Green Glass Surface, Düsseldorf 1995-96

The broken lance of the project for an international art museum on Lanzarote (1999) is a gesture. It stands as a very direct translation of a local myth according to which Joan de Bethencourt, one of the first colonists, received the message of the island's capitulation and out of joy over the news threw his lance which broke apart when it landed. As opposed to the abstract application of the metaphor in the Neanderthal Museum, the broken lance can be seen as being similar to Venturi's duck, even though the structure does not express its contents through its appearance. Conceived as a huge tower with a viewing platform on top, reached by a cable way, the building does not leave much room for speculation. It is the broken lance. In order to communicate the island's identity, Zamp Kelp draws back to the rules of representational art. An object is taken and represented in such a manner that it can easily be recognised and communicate its message.

The incorporation of client images and logos into the design of facades is another strategy that Zamp Kelp employs to create identity. The Neanderthal Museum, the Millennium View and the broken lance are three-dimensional objects that communicate their stories through their shape and materials. The project for the entrance area of the E Plus headquarters in Düsseldorf makes use of existing imagery and treats the building's facades as huge billboards. The similarity between the lance on Lanzarote and the flock of birds in Düsseldorf is that they are recognisable objects and images. In the case of the lance, though, we are dealing with an object that has been translated into another scale and medium. The flock of birds has been derived from an image. When we look at the facade of E Plus, we do not associate birds but the logo of the firm. It is here that Baudrillard's doubt over the reference principle between object and image might be at its most applicable, since we might have reached a point were a flock of live birds reminds us of the logo of E Plus. Thus the objective of the creation of identity for E Plus has been achieved.

perception / authenticity / translocation / virtuality

Visual perception, the problem of authenticity and the phenomenon of translocation are strongly interlinked. According to Zamp Kelp, the phenomenon of translocation consists of 'the trinity of place, event and the transport of media'. Since the duality of event and place has been extended by the transport of media, and thus the mediated experience, perception and the question of authenticity become relevant for the production of architecture. At the same time as we are dealing with the object, we are dealing with its mediated image. The image has become more important than the object. The importance lies in our understanding of this very phenomenon.

The opposition of object / place and image has been explored by Zamp Kelp in various ways. In his design for the Ornamenta 1 jewellery exhibition in Pforzheim (1989), for instance, he directly opposed image and object. In the Mekka Medial project for Paris, the space was mediated by the event and the transport of information to a different location.

Projections, according to Zamp Kelp, play a major part in our perception, especially in the urban environment. They have also altered our understanding of the notion of what is private and what is public space. The private has become public; our private space, for example our living room, is constantly exposed to media projections, whether through television, newspapers or commodities that no longer stand for a quality or function, but for the corporations that produce them. We now need to invent new mechanisms to reinstate our privacy. These are not spatial means necessarily but will rather be found in behavioural patterns, once we have learned to live with the changed conditions. This also means that we have to become accustomed to and accept projections as an opportunity to create space.

Haus-Rucker-Co experimented with the notion of psychological space in a number of projects in the Mind Expanding Programme, which was aimed at a totally new and different psychological and physical experience. One important aspect of this programme was the investigation of an alteration of visual perception. All the projects were based on the premise that they had to be used in order to achieve the desired effects for the individual's perception. In this sense they could be seen as mini-environments, but at the same time users were exposed to a kind of experience that took them into a different realm. Thus it was not the actual installation of the project or its aesthetic appearance, but the way in which it manipulated one's perception of a certain situation that was important. In these respects, the Mind Expanding Programme was similar to the way that the helmets for virtual reality experiences work. Even though Zamp Kelp is not designing spaces for virtual reality, the notion of the virtual and its omnipresence through electronic media has been manifested in almost all his projects.

surface / texture

The envelope of a building as its physical public face is one of Zamp Kelp's main concerns. Even though, due to projected information into the private sphere, he doubts the value of opaque building materials as protectors for privacy, the envelope and edge of a building play an important role in the way that they are the physical means of communication with the outside world.

Zamp Kelp's idea of the facade as an independent medium has its origins in different sources. It goes back, via Le Corbusier's five points of architecture, to the idea of the mask, originating in Vienna at the turn of the twentieth century. Although both origins seemingly imply the same consequence, namely that the skin of a building is independent from the building's structure, they differ in their individual interpretation of the problem. The idea of the mask is concerned with the question of identity, or rather hiding and revealing multiple identities. Although this has spatial implications, it has no obvious relevance for construction and thus the mask is a concept that does not need to be articulated in terms of a separation of structure and facade. Le Corbusier's five points of architecture contained the articulation of the facade as a separate element from the structure. Zamp Kelp's treatment of the surface falls between both ideas, but is in some ways more closely related to the notion of mask since it does not rely on the separation between skin and structure as a conceptual means. This also implies that his treatment of surface, operating with both abstract and figurative means, is somehow situated between that of modernism and postmodernism. What distinguishes Zamp Kelp's work from the Modern Movement is that even when he applies materials in an abstract fashion, the material itself is expressive and he tries to establish a relationship with the task at hand and the applied material. The surface becomes a sign, translating Venturi's lesson's from *Learning from Las Vegas*. However, while postmodernism denies

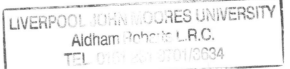

Zamp Kelp and J.Krauss / A.Brandlhuber: Neanderthal Museum, Mettmann, 1994-96, 1:1 Model of Facade

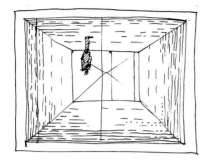

Zamp Kelp: Zero-Gravity Space, Düsseldorf 1998-99

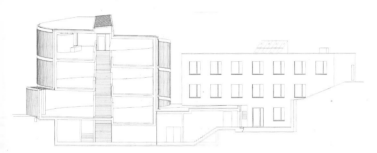

Zamp Kelp and J.Krauss / A.Brandlehuber:
Neanderthal Museum,
Mettmann, 1994-96, Section

Zamp Kelp: Expanding Space,
Meinerzhagen, 1992, Model

the metanarrative, Zamp Kelp uses metaphor, and thus narrative, to generate his designs. Because he is fully aware of this conflict, the contradiction in the work becomes its strength. It is interesting to note that although Zamp Kelp pursues specific aims and interpretations of the world, his narratives are open to multiple readings and suggestions.

In the first Haus-Rucker-Co project, the Ballon Für Zwei, construction, skin, surface and material all became one and the same thing in the form of the PVC membrane. At the same time, the membrane was the medium through which the urban environment was perceived.

Surface has since become a key term in many contemporary architects' vocabularies, though it is not always clear whether surface is regarded only as a visual means – as in the case of projections like television and advertising – or whether it is used as a tactile means to explore physical qualities. Zamp Kelp's understanding of the significance of surface for our perception of the urban environment has led him to various conclusions. His treatment of surfaces – both internal and external – often refers to specific places and circumstances while at the same time employing a high degree of abstraction. The question of surface is linked to the problem of distinguishing between abstract and figurative expression.

Zamp Kelp relies on surface as a signifier of messages. Depending on the individual project, he applies materials in either an abstract manner or as imagery. The surface or skin of a building, as seen by Zamp Kelp, is always a carrier of information. Information as such can occur in various ways. Since we live in an age where information about an event or an object has become more important than the thing itself, the medium through which the information is transported has gained an important role. Thus a new 'object hood' of the medium is being established.

Zamp Kelp has not established a hierarchy of materials: all materials have the same value to begin with. This allows him to apply them in unconventional ways, thus providing both building and material with new readings. The way that he uses individual materials reveals a keen interest in building technology, though technology is never used as an end in itself. Rather, it is Zamp Kelp's curiosity and willingness to experiment with materials, to test their expression when used in different circumstances, that show his fascination with modern technology.

Zamp Kelp has experimented a great deal with glass and its three main visual qualities – transparency, translucency, opaqueness – as a material in which to wrap his buildings. Glass provides him with the opportunity to play with imagery and to explore the depth of the building's skin. While on the one hand he creates very flat physical surfaces, on the other he raises the question of where the skin starts and where it ends. The facade of the Neanderthal Museum, clad in industrial glazing panels, is a flat, abstract surface but it is also a series of layers which reveals the building's structure. The abstract nature of the facade allows viewers to project their own interpretations and thoughts on to the building. At the same time, Zamp Kelp achieves a sensual material quality, manifesting the object character of the facade on location.

In the project for the International Art Museum on Lanzarote, the surface of the raised slab is treated as a piece of island and is clad in local volcanic stone. Here, surface directly takes on the meaning of one specific material. Even though this could be seen as a rather simplistic way of dealing with the building's skin, the position of the slab 8m in the air, hovering over a dug-out piece of the site, transfers the volcanic stone into another realm. Zamp Kelp uses the technique of the cut to express qualities in a material that would otherwise remain hidden. The two conditions of the volcanic stone, as rock and as manufactured cladding material, are shown next to each other.

The application of imagery, in an abstract or figurative manner, is another strategic means employed frequently by Zamp Kelp. Again, he explores glass as a carrier for images and information in various different ways. In the project for the entrance facade and lobby for the E Plus Communications company, the glass wall and the logo become one, so the distinction between architecture and sign does not exist. The architecture is a sign and vice versa. In his proposal for House

"It is Zamp Kelp's understanding of the value of the surface as both carrier of information and object that allows him to create a sense of uniqueness in each of his projects.Behind a River Landscape, Düsseldorf, 1992, imagery is applied to the facade of the building in a different way. The local river landscape is screen print-ed on to the glass panels that clad the building. Thus an overlay of image and exist-ing landscape is achieved, again exploring the relationship between object and image".

The city, according to Zamp Kelp, is perceived through its surfaces. This does not mean that the public face of a building has to express its contents. Zamp Kelp is interested in the effects that certain materials, strategically used, have on our visual perception. The use of Dadaist techniques in order to explore the complex relationship between objects has in these respects not changed since his early work with Haus-Rucker-Co.[44] His aims remain much as they did in one of Haus-Rucker-Co's manifestos: to crack old and unchallenged habits of visual perception. Zamp Kelp has extended this statement in his recent work with the objective that his archi-tecture should serve as a means to gain a better understanding of the world.

Notes

1 Charles Baudelaire, *The Painter of Modern Life* (published in 1863), in Charles Baudelaire, *Selected Writings on Art and Artists*, London, 1981; quoted in David Harvey, *The Condition of Postmodernity*, Basil Blackwell, Oxford, 1990, p10.

2 Haus-Rucker-Co was a group of Austrian architects and artists that was founded by Günter Zamp Kelp, Laurids Ortner and Klaus Pinter in 1967 in Vienna and from 1971 included Manfred Ortner. In 1970 the group moved to Düsseldorf in Germany (later it also had a studio in Berlin). In 1972 Haus-Rucker-Inc was established as an independent group in New York by Klaus Pinter and Carroll Michels. In 1977 Haus-Rucker-Inc broke up as a group: Pinter and Michels carried on as an inde-pendent artist and a freelance journalist respectively. In 1987 Manfred and Laurids Ortner founded the practice Ortner Architekten (since 1990: Ortner & Ortner) and Zamp Kelp established his own architectural practice in Düsseldorf. In 1992 Haus-Rucker-Co officially ceased to exist.

3 Stanislaus von Moos, 'Kunst und Technik: Direktkoppelungen', in Heinrich Klotz (ed), *Haus-Rucker-Co 1967-1983*, Vieweg, Braunschweig/Wiesbaden, 1984. In this essay Stanislaus von Moos reflects on Haus-Rucker-Co's work from an architectural historian's point of view, following Haus-Rucker-Co's precedents through the fifties (Alison and Peter Smithson, Archigram, The Situationnistes), the twenties and thirties (Dada and Surrealism) back to Russian Constructivism and Futurism in the first two decades of the twentieth century.

4 Dieter Bogner, *Denkräume – Stadträume*, Ritter Verlag, Klagenfurt, 1992. Dieter Bogner describes Haus-Rucker-Co's projects and examines how they were conceived and perceived from the sixties onwards.

5 Stanislaus von Moos, 'Kunst und Technik: Direktkoppelungen', in Heinrich Klotz (ed), *Haus-Rucker-Co 1967-1983, op.cit*, p7.

6 Jonathan Raban, *Soft City*, Hamish Hamilton, Middlesex, 1974, p9.

7 The German philosopher Walter Benjamin remains a strong source for Zamp Kelp.

8 As Von Moos points out, Haus-Rucker-Co were some of the first architects to incorporate the lessons of Venturi's *Learning from Las Vegas* into their work.

9 '...Handke was insulting his audience. Hollein and Pichler held their exhibition on "Architekturin" the Galerie nächst Sankt Stephan...Hermann Czech was writing in the furrow.' Günter Zamp Kelp, 'Journal', in Heinrich Klotz (ed), *Haus-Rucker-Co 1967-1983, op.cit*, p31.

10 'A colossal monument should cause our excitement in order to convince us ... of its extra-ord inariness. Its greatness should put everything around it in the shade. In its uniqueness it must re-present a great idea of its kind.' Etienne-Louis Boullée, *Architecture, Treatise on the Arts*, quoted in Günter Zamp Kelp, 'Vom Monument zum Ereignis', in *Kunst als Revolte*, ed. K Wilhelm, Anabas Verlag, 1996, p143.

11 Ibid.

12 In the same exhibition, the then more established Hans Hollein, Günter Domenig and Eilfried Huth also showed their work.

13 Laurids Ortner, 'Zu Nevem Raum', in Klotz (ed), *Haus-Rucker-Co 1967-1983*, p71.

14 Dieter Bogner, *Denkräume – Stadträume, op.cit*, p275.

15 Archigram were Warren Chalk, Peter Cook, Dennis Crompton, David Green, Ron Herron and Mike Webb. Archigram first appeared in the public eye with the publication of *archigram 1* in 1961.

16 Günter Zamp Kelp, 'Journal', in Heinrich Klotz (ed),*Haus-Rucker-Co 1967-1983*, p36.

17 Ibid, p37.

18 'Günter Zamp Kelp in Conversation with Torsten Schmiedeknecht', *Architectural Design*, Profile No 135, 9/10 1988, p46.

19 In much of his later work, Zamp Kelp dwells on the necessity of raising an awareness in urban inhab-itants of their environment. In an earlier Haus-Rucker-Co text the bridging of the gap in the devel-opment of our body, still being that of the nineteenth century, and our mind, being exposed to phe-nomena of perception already belonging to the twenty-first century is identified as a key issue.

20 Hans Hollein, *Absolute Architecture*, Catalogue of the Hollein-Pichler exhibition, Galerie Nächst Sankt Stephan, Vienna, 1963. (Taken from: U Conrads (ed), *Programs and Manifestos on 20th Century Architecture*, MIT Press, Cambridge, Mass.1971, trans Michael Bullock, p182.)

21 These terms are of specific interest when looking at Zamp Kelp's contemporary work.

22 This thought was equally pursued by Archigram at the same time.

23 After Achleitner left the group, partly to become a writer and critic, it was known as the 'Dreiviertler', as in three-four-time (Viennese waltz).

24 It has been pointed out before that Haus-Rucker-Co had a very strong belief in the power of technology as a means to transform society.

25 'Mind Expanding Programme. Technological achievements of our time are way ahead of our intellectual and physical development. We are human beings of the eighteenth and nineteenth centuries and have to live in shapes of the twentieth and twenty-first centuries.

For the moment it seems to be impossible to apply the large amount of constantly occurring scientific discoveries and results to simple daily life. Like an explosion the development is going towards the outside, the direction towards man and the inside of man remains neglected. MEP is aimed to explore the Inner-Space, the space inside man, and to discover and develop psy-phy forces. MEP creates an alphabet of aggressive moulding. Shapes develop aggressive energies that have a psychological and physical impact on man. The amount of energy increases with the size of the shape. Directed mass-form creates total change in human life. Cities are our biggest radiators of energy. Still undirected today their impact on human life will be precisely determined and of exact measure.' Haus-Rucker-Co in Dieter Bogner, *Denkräume – Stadträume, op.cit*, p39.

26 Stanilaus von Moos, for instance, draws a parallel between the Haus-Rucker-Co projects like Giant Billard and Moholy Nagy's and Farkas Molnar's experiments around the subject of the Total Theatre.

27 Constant Nieuwenhuis quoted in Stanislaus von Moos, 'Kunst und Technic: Directkoppelungen' in Klotz (ed), *Haus-Rucker-Co 1967-1983*, p8.

28 Oase No.7, was an inflatable transparent PVC sphere installed at the Documenta 5 in Kassel in 1972.

29 Catalogue *This is Tomorrow*, group 6 section. The project consisted of a shed structure that was contained within reflective walls, thus creating a total environment in which Henderson and Paolozzi installed their objects.

30 Archigram, extract from *Living Arts Magazine*, No 2, June 1963, quoted in *Archigram*, Peter Cook (ed) with Warren Chalk, Dennis Crompton, David Greene, Ron Herron and Mike Webb, Birkhäuser, Basel, 1991, p20.

31 Dieter Bogner, *Denkräume – Stadträume, op.cit*, p274.

32 'In the current consciousness and reality, city and nature are an opposed pair, fighting each other. The laws of nature are being confronted with the expanding chaos of urban civilisation. The conceptual extension of both realms with the term "landscape" shifts the opposed notions and makes them into parts of an entirety that substantially changes the position of nature in our awareness. The landscapes of nature and city become part of a whole that we could call the landscape of culture, or "cultural landscape".' Zamp Kelp,' Dynamik der Leere', *Kunstzeitschrift*, March 1985, p41.

33 Jean Baudrillard, *The Evil Demon of Images* (trans Paul Patton and Paul Foss), The Power Institute of Fine Arts, University of Sydney,1987, p16.

34 Beatriz Colomina observes in her book *Privacy and Publicity*, 'The railway transforms the world into a commodity. It makes places into objects of consumption and, in doing so, deprives them of their quality as places. Oceans, mountains, and cities float in the world just like the objects of universal exhibitions ... Photography does for architecture what the railway did for cities, transforming it into merchandise and conveying it through the magazines for it to be consumed by the masses.' Beatriz Colomina, *Privacy and Publicity*, MIT Press, Cambridge, Mass., 1994; fourth reprint,1998, p47.

35 Jean Baudrillard, *The Evil Demon of Images* p13.

36 Marshall McLuhan, *Understanding Media*, 1964; reprinted by MIT Press, Cambridge, Mass., 1994, p124.

37 Adolf Loos, *Architektur* (1910); quoted in Beatriz Colomina, *Privacy and Publicity,* p68.

38 Dan Graham, *Rock My Religion*, art/design/urbanism, MIT Press, Cambridge, Mass.,1993, p254.

39 *Collins English Dictionary,* Collins, London and Glasgow, 1988.

40 Ibid.

41 Ibid.

42 In the fifties and sixties Alison and Peter Smithson, Archigram and Haus-Rucker-Co rediscovered the everyday for architecture. Paradoxically, fine art, in the form of Dadaism, Surrealism and Pop Art, had also tried to bridge the gap from the museum to everyday life. Naturally, none of these movements could overcome their own existence as avant-garde and thus they have all long since returned to the museum. In architecture, Robert Venturi made the everyday popular in the seventies. But it is only in the late nineties that the everyday was once again rediscovered, particularly in contemporary European architecture.

43 Heinrich Klotz, *Die Revision Der Moderne*, Prestel Verlag, Munich, and DAM, Frankfurt, 1984, p10.

44 Stanislaus von Moos commented that Haus-Rucker-Co's 'Rahmenbau' project for the 1977 Documenta in Kassel was the reverse of Duchamp's readymades, since it put a piece of everyday industrial landscape on display. The staircase building of the Millennium View and the viewing box in the Neanderthal Museum are both further developments of this idea.

Sixties, Las Vegas and Snow White

Torsten Schmiedeknecht in conversation with Paul Davies

Paul Davies

Archigram: Walking City, Ron Herron, 1964

Las Vegas, Bellagio Under Construction

Torsten Schmiedeknecht   You are fascinated by Las Vegas and have also conducted research into the relationship between architecture and film, both in terms of meaning and production. Also, you are interested in the cultural relevance of the sixties. Zamp Kelp approaches architecture from a different angle, but he shares quite a few of your fascinations. He is interested in how film and television have altered our understanding of space and objects; in surface and sign as architecture; and he used to be part of the international avant-garde, if the term avant-garde is still relevant. Could you please tell me what your fascination is with Las Vegas?

Paul Davies   On one level I suppose there's the idea that Las Vegas represents the world which Archigram predicted in the sixties, in the sense that Las Vegas is that great moving, ever-changing city.˙ Ten per cent of any casino will be undergoing change as we speak. And once you've opened a casino, you don't shut it, because they're open 24 hours a day, so it runs forever. It really is that flux of human activity that was so beloved of a generation, lasting from, say, 1960 to 1972. As regards my own fascination, I love architectures that are prescribed or designed to please. There are amazing specialists who conjure up these environments with only one aim in mind: to give pleasure – and, of course, to extort a certain amount of money from your pocket over a three-day average stay. It's a capitalist environment. There are some people who find that appalling and they take a resistive approach to what architecture should be. My particular interest in Archigram led me to think that perhaps one should not be so judgmental and that these processes are going on any way, no matter what. Remember Marshall McLuhan. He said: 'I don't like anything that I talk about but I'm still telling you that it's happening'. Therefore it's worthy of study. If you can build a 3,000-room casino in 18 months that's a pretty cool thing to do.

TS   The pleasures you're talking about, at what kind of level do they take place? Are they physical or visual?

PD   They're certainly visual; they're certainly sensory. Going to Las Vegas is like getting into a big warm bath. They're not the pleasures you get from looking at a Joseph Beuys work of art or an Anselm Kiefer painting. They are much more to do with a recognition of iconic things in culture, recreated in different media, from film to building to active sculpture to souvenir to t-shirt to child's toy all jumbled up together.

TS   I seem to remember that in a lecture once you spoke about the change that has taken place in Las Vegas since Venturi evaluated it in *Learning from Las Vegas*.

PD   A lot of people associate Las Vegas – quite rightly – with a sort of sixties brat pack image; Frank Sinatra, Dean Martin and all the rest of it. Robert Venturi visited in 1968 and published *Learning from Las Vegas* in 1972. His fascination was really with what he called 'the everyday' or 'main street is almost all right', and he saw Las Vegas as the most extreme version of popular culture – people doing their own thing without artists and architects.

Haus-Rucker-Co: Environment Transformer, 1968

Las Vegas, Poolside at the Rio

TS   Coming back to that idea of pleasure: the early Haus-Rucker-Co work was somehow about direct pleasure as well. It was about exposing you to something that would make you perceive your environment in a different way or make you aware of things that otherwise you wouldn't have seen. It was also about intensification. The Environment Transformers or the Yellow Heart, for instance, made you visually perceive your environment through a membrane. Would you say that what's happening in Las Vegas in terms of intensification is a similar thing; that, for instance, you can experience things in Las Vegas in a way that you can't in South London?

PD   That's quite hard to say. Obsession with trying to heighten experience seems to be a common thing in architecture. The number of times students say: 'I've observed such and such in that street and I want to intensify it.' But they usually mean and do it in a highly abstract way and thus the product becomes highly abstract. Las Vegas does not work in an abstract way; it works in a highly, over-concentrated figurative way and therefore uses iconic imagery and tends to be loud. Even when it's trying to be sophisticated, it is the most luscious sophistication possible.

TS   But it's 2D, isn't it. Zamp Kelp also pursues the intensification in a spatial way. And the argument there is: why should I simulate anything? I am going to intensify what's here anyway, which then brings the question of programme into play. What do you make of the programme? Do you start theming it? And how do you do it? With the Neanderthal Museum, for instance, one could say that Zamp Kelp was theming it, even if it was in a metaphorical way. So how do you go about designing a casino?

PD   My definition of theming would be that if you go for a popular medium such as television or film and you translate it into a built environment, the archetypal representation of that is Disneyland. It is the archetypal starting point for a discussion between film and architecture in my opinion – which is the one, of course, that most people ignore. What interests me about the work of Zamp Kelp is that his concern with projections and screens is an abstraction. So there are two different strategies you find today. The more apparent one is that you start off with *Snow White and the Seven Dwarfs*, which is an amazing film, and you end up with the design of a screen in a public square. As opposed to that you have the Disney model, which is to try and flesh out the characters to story board, to myth make, to build storytelling environments.

TS   What about Zamp Kelp's project for Lanzarote?

PD   That project strikes me as being a combination of two different genres. One is: I am an architect and I am interested in conceptual art. The other is: I am an architect and I'm interested in the relationship between stories and myth and identity, and I need to represent that in some kind of monument. Both things happen at the same time. Let's remember, for an architect starting out in the early sixties, there's a huge tension – whether an architect could be an artist, or whether an architect should be a designer. The designer would perhaps hold much greater possibilities. Reyner Banham talks about keeping up with technology or joining the club of architects. At the same time, Charles Eames always loved to be called an architect and not a designer because he liked the heritage associated with the word architect. In America, the word architect was cherished whereas in England everybody wanted to become a designer. The options in the sixties where much broader – in terms of getting along in your life – than we have now in our sort of 'super capitalism' where you do have to feed the kids and send them to school. You can't do that on no fees. People like Peter Zumthor, who started his career in a non-urban environment, for instance, had different parameters. He could develop that persona of the hermit, which of course now everybody has capitalised on, to write about and make him famous. For most people involved in urban investigations in the sixties, the economic difficulties of living in the city caught up with them

Las Vegas does not work in an abstract way; it works in a highly, over-concentrated figurative way and therefore uses iconic imagery and tends to be loud. Even when it's trying to be sophisticated, it is the most luscious sophistication possible.

much quicker. The real possibilities of what architecture is were soon reduced to: I am going to be an artist and I'm going to be poor, or, I am going to be commercial and get building commissions. Architecture has always been this combination. Is it art? Is it commerce? Is it craftsmanship? Is it philosophy? Those things were wide open in the sixties.

TS Was it that people were less interested in the definition?

PD The whole horizon was opened up in the sixties massively. You had somebody landing on the moon; you had 500,000 people camping out in a field and leaving it empty within the next day. You had a whole raft of revolutionary movements which were changing governments. There really was a wave of change.

TS But these effects carried on into the early eighties, with the Green Movement and so on ...

PD The question for me is really whether you look at Zamp Kelp's buildings in a tradition that flows smoothly from the work of the sixties or whether it is down to a series of external conditions which demanded that the architects from this particular generation either went and built or went into teaching.

TS Zamp Kelp is an interesting case in these respects. He was teaching in the early Haus-Rucker-Co days in Vienna. In the eighties, he replaced Ungers at Cornell for a term and he has now been a professor in Berlin for about ten years. But his ambition is and always has been to build, to manufacture the things that he is drawing. Archigram, for instance, were into the production of ideas but not objects. The majority of Haus-Rucker-Co projects were executed; they were really into testing their ideas.

PD I think also in the sixties there was this feeling that you could do anything.

TS But most of these things were of course reactions to existing circumstances. In the sixties, you could still be shocking and provocative. Who and how are you going to shock today? The possibilities for supposedly individual self-expression seem to be so much more. Of course, it's all organised and the moment anything semi-radical seems to develop, it gets bought up by some clever marketing guy.

PD That brings us back to Las Vegas. We clearly don't live in a world like in 1968 where Reyner Banham would tell us what popular culture meant and instruct the groovy people at the AA or Hornsey School of Art on how to appreciate a Ford Mustang, or explain why Barbarella was so important when she slept in a polythene bag. We don't live in that world because we've got so many media critics; we've got so much media; and we choose our own venue within the whole breadth of culture. Cultural critics now tend to be very cynical, very funny. They do not educate; they entertain. Architects and their critics, though, seem to have become sober and serious. I think that we've lost some of the fun that was there in the sixties. Putting that bubble on the side of a building, I mean, that's great fun. It's just for the sheer enjoyment, and we'd all be there giggling. I think things are very different now.

TS Yes and no. In Zamp Kelp's work I see a continuous line. The recent work is about space, of course, but it's also about surface. Las Vegas is about surface and nothing else in a way ...

PD ... cream cake surface.

TS The first bubble and the Neanderthal Museum are closely related. It's all about perception, about the perception of your environment. Haus-Rucker-Co were the ones who said, we're accepting the urban environment as it is. One of the manifestos was even called 'Amnesty for the Built Reality' ...

PD   Fantastic. That's very much in line with somebody like Robert Smithson, when he wrote those monumental essays about what one might consider awful or ordinary places, like New Jersey, because suddenly everything was interesting. The fascination for me is that if you do accept the world where everything is interesting – of course many critics might say, we're appalled, you've lost your sense of values and so on – it would miraculously change architectural education. Robert Smithson has huge consequences if you take him seriously. He is very relevant because he redirected people's vision.

TS   Some of the Haus-Rucker-Co stuff was very much in that tradition, I would say.

PD   Which in Zamp Kelp's work has now resulted in this notion of projection. In the Neanderthal Museum, I would say it comes down to skins and light – translucency. In other projects, it manifests itself in screens. There always seems to be that notion of the projection of the self, something extremely internal. The term projection seems to link up these superficially different types of work. Looking at the way that the early and the recent work could be connected, there is something particularly interesting about a tradition which starts from the premiss that everything can change. There was a tremendously difficult metaphorical dimension with drawings in the sixties. Was it a potato? Was it a spaceship? Was it finished? How could you draw change? What seems to remain is a certain way of thinking about programme, in a sense that in the sixties defining the strategy to approach something was the aim. That was the ultimate goal. The Nirvana was not to do any work but to have the perfect strategy. Some of us might say that this should still be the way to work today. Students today can usually do very nice graphics but they are not very good strategically; in fact, they are very poor strategic thinkers. In the sixties, programme did mean a lot and there were a lot of discussions about how programme inhabited architecture. So inevitably, when Zamp Kelp came to design a museum, he must have thought very carefully about it. What I like very much about the drawings of the Neanderthal Museum is that they are very plain, in a tradition of the drawings of the competition scheme for, say, the Berlin Free University. They are diagrams and diagrams are the cipher for the analysis of programme.

Paris, Las Vegas

TS   What's the programme in Las Vegas?

PD   The programme in Las Vegas is to wheedle as much money out of people's pockets as is possible in three days. That's what creates the architecture. That's the problem with some of Venturi's points. He says that he's not interested in the programmatic elements of Las Vegas's buildings. He says he's not interested in the moral world that surrounds it. But I don't know many main streets which rely on 15 million slot machines in order to get their vital energy to keep going as main streets. Even though I really love *Learning from Las Vegas*, this is the one point where Venturi had to skip around, because he was working in an environment in the sixties where you couldn't enjoy such low-class culture as gambling and whoring. Now, due to our lifestyle culture, we live in a world where you can be respected and have a reputation for all those 'bad' things.

TS   How does that relate to the notion of identity? Zamp Kelp has this theory that cities, more than ever before, are competing with each other.

PD   Yes, cities are competing with each other, mainly for customers, for the dollar in your pocket. Travel has become very much part of our world. And because you need your fix of safety and identity when you travel, the qualities of cities or destination environments have to be fairly heightened. If I go to the Carribean, I

Fantastic. That's very much in line with somebody like Robert Smithson, when he wrote those monumental essays about what one might consider awful or ordinary places, like New Jersey, because suddenly everything was interesting... Robert Smithson has huge consequences if you take him seriously.

need that Caribbean experience in three days or a week. So time, travel and speed are important in the construction of identity, because the further you travel and the less time you spend there, the more concentrated the experience has to be, to be a satisfactory one – unless you are the sort of lone wolf traveller. But there aren't many people who don't want things they have seen on TV because it's pretty hard not to be influenced by the media.

TS   Zamp Kelp is saying that to create the scenarios you just mentioned, the projected space could be used on location, which I suppose is what's happening in Las Vegas.

PD   We have to differentiate, though, between types of projection. When it comes to public art for instance, Las Vegas doesn't understand what public art is. It has done public art forever and a day but it's never called it public art. There's no conception in Las Vegas of what art is.

TS   If you took the projections away from Las Vegas, which seems to me to consist of a mixture of 3D iconographic symbols and their projections ...

PD   The world's biggest TV screen is in the MGM Grand, where you sit minuscule on your bar stool in front of a four-storey high screen showing James Bond films.

TS   So does that not heighten the experience of Las Vegas?

PD   It certainly does.

TS   So they are doing what Zamp Kelp is talking about?

PD   I would like to go to Las Vegas with Zamp Kelp and I think we'd have a great time. We are talking about a world beyond taste here. It is not the question whether Las Vegas is good taste or bad taste ...

TS   No, it's about the means that are being employed.

Zamp Kelp is saying that to create the scenarios you just mentioned, the projected space could be used on location, which I suppose is what's happening in Las Vegas.

Las Vegas Strip by Night

Certainly, Las Vegas utilises projection in every single form, even to the point of surreal kind of juxtapositions of the same, if you include projection in its widest sense.

I agree with you. Even in pre-television times, there's always been the mediated experience. There's always been mediation. The church, for instance, used to be a great mediator. There have always been people to tell you what or what not to do or to think. The Cheers Bar is, in these respects, not so dissimilar to religion.

PD   Certainly, Las Vegas utilises projection in every single form, even to the point of surreal kind of juxtapositions of the same, if you include projection in it's widest sense. In Zamp Kelp's work there are all sorts of different applications of projections, like the projection of the self or cinematic projections. But we could use projection as a metaphor for bringing Siberian white tigers to the middle of the Nevada desert in 150 degrees of heat.

TS   When I think about projections Baudrillard always comes to mind, since projection and simulation are somehow related.

PD   With regards to simulation and Jean Baudrillard, there is always a kind of melancholic loss which seems to be implied. With Baudrillard having been a Marxist in 1968, there's always this notion about things not having been achieved. In Baudrillard's case, this becomes particularly acute when he goes to America. We read every day in the media that the most overwhelming experience in America is that people become a different person every day. So it is no surprise that Baudrillard says that this simulation world is somehow the real world. In my opinion, it is interesting in the most obvious example of the simulated world, or rather the one that is most often confused with it: the filmic world. If you look at television, there are deep layers of history in the manufacture of ephemeral images. So one could say with something like the Cheers Bar, that there are at least five or six levels of history or archaeology to the bar itself as an object. There's a rumour that the bar is beneath the sound stage at Paramount, were it was originally filmed, ready to be reconstructed if they ever did another series. There is a truncated version of the so-called real bar in the Hollywood Film Museum – it's got three feet missing from the middle because they couldn't get it into the room – and crowds of school children go and worship at it. And in the place, where nobody knows your name, at airports, you've got all the replica Cheers Bars which don't look like Cheers Bars because often they'll be a different form. And then back in the original town, in Boston, there are two Cheers Bars. One is not called Cheers Bar because it was the original inspiration and then there's a special Cheers Bar made as a replica of that. So as opposed to Baudrillard, I was not melancholic at all, I was enthused by the wealth of history and interpretation that was available within this particular arena.

TS   I agree with you. Even in pre-television times, there's always been the mediated experience. There's always been mediation. The church, for instance, used to be a great mediator. There have always been people to tell you what or what not to do or to think. The Cheers Bar is, in these respects, not so dissimilar to religion.

PD   It would be quite exciting to write an article comparing the Cheers Bar and some particular religious artifact, shifted across continents to different locations and displayed in different ways. So really, all I am trying to say with regard to Jean Baudrillard is hold on a minute, these objects might be seen in a different perspective.

TS   So what about the physical space?

PD   In my view, everything that Archigram stood for has come true. It just doesn't look like Archigram.

TS   Which brings us back to the generational shift, I suppose.

PD   There is a good story about the Smithsons tracing all these 'family trees' of architects: the group who worked on Corb's Unité who then went on to build the Berlin Free University, the next generation of which went on to build – I don't know – whatever. I think the interesting thing about the generation from 1960 was, like

I think the most authentic place that you can be in at the end of the twentieth century is in your seat on an aeroplane, with a wonderful selection of TV, headphones on, listening to something else and gazing out of the window as the earth slides beneath your wing tips.

Archigram and Haus-Rucker-Co, it came from nowhere; it was student led. And that whole fashion that we have now for transgressing boundaries was well in evidence in the sixties.

TS   So how does that go together with that sudden urge – which can't just be a reaction against modernism – that everything has to be about identity again and that place becomes important again. Everything that modernism had denied or negated.

PD   I think that it's a bit of a German thing, though.

TS   No.

PD   You don't think so.

TS   No, I think it's particularly in the British education system that the phenomenologists are dominant.

PD   I think the most authentic place that you can be in at the end of the twentieth century is in your seat on an aeroplane, with a wonderful selection of TV, headphones on, listening to something else and gazing out of the window as the earth slides beneath your wing tips.

TS   But in a world of brands, identity is maybe not so much to be seen in the phenomenological sense but more in quite a straightforward fashion, that I buy what I recognise.

PD   I have certain bars in Las Vegas where I go as soon as I get off the plane because they are my centres of identity.

TS   But you knew what you were looking for in Las Vegas.

PD   Yes. You always know what you're going to find before you get it. There's a marvellous moment of recognition, when you've found that particular bar, on the outskirts of Las Vegas, full of Cowboys or something, and you're going yes, and they're playing Van Halen in the juke box, and you go yes: I'm here; I've got what I wanted. And that's a marvellous revelation.
London, Southbank University, 3 June 1999.

* The idea of the ever-changing 'play city' had also been pursued by Haus-Rucker-Co in the sixties and seventies and was part of their strategy to overcome the gap between art and life.

Paul Davies is senior lecturer in the architecture of tourism at South Bank University and at the Architectural Association, London. He visits Las Vegas, his favourite city, as a matter of habit, or perhaps addiction, whenever possible.
   He has written widely for *Building Design*, *Blueprint*, and *FX* magazines, and the academic *Journal of Architecture*. Three further essays discuss contemporary Las Vegas: 'Tales of Vicarious Consumption: Hollywood's (Living Room)' History in *Architectural Design*, 'Consuming Architecture'; Just Add Water in 'Vertigo, The Strange New World of The Contemporary City' and The Landscape of Luxury in 'Occupying Architecture'.

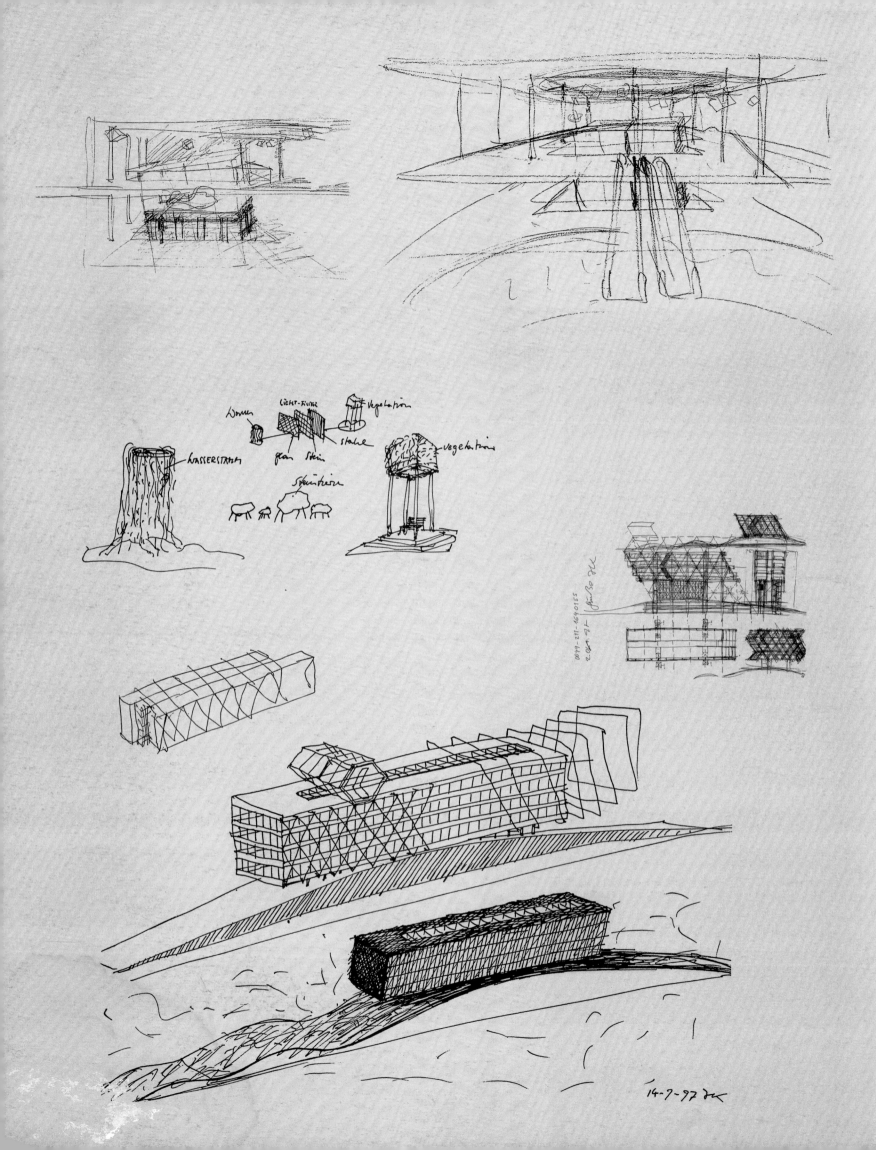

Wasser

Licht-Fuge   Vegetation

Wasserstand

stahle

glas Stein

Steinkörse

Vegetation

14-7-97

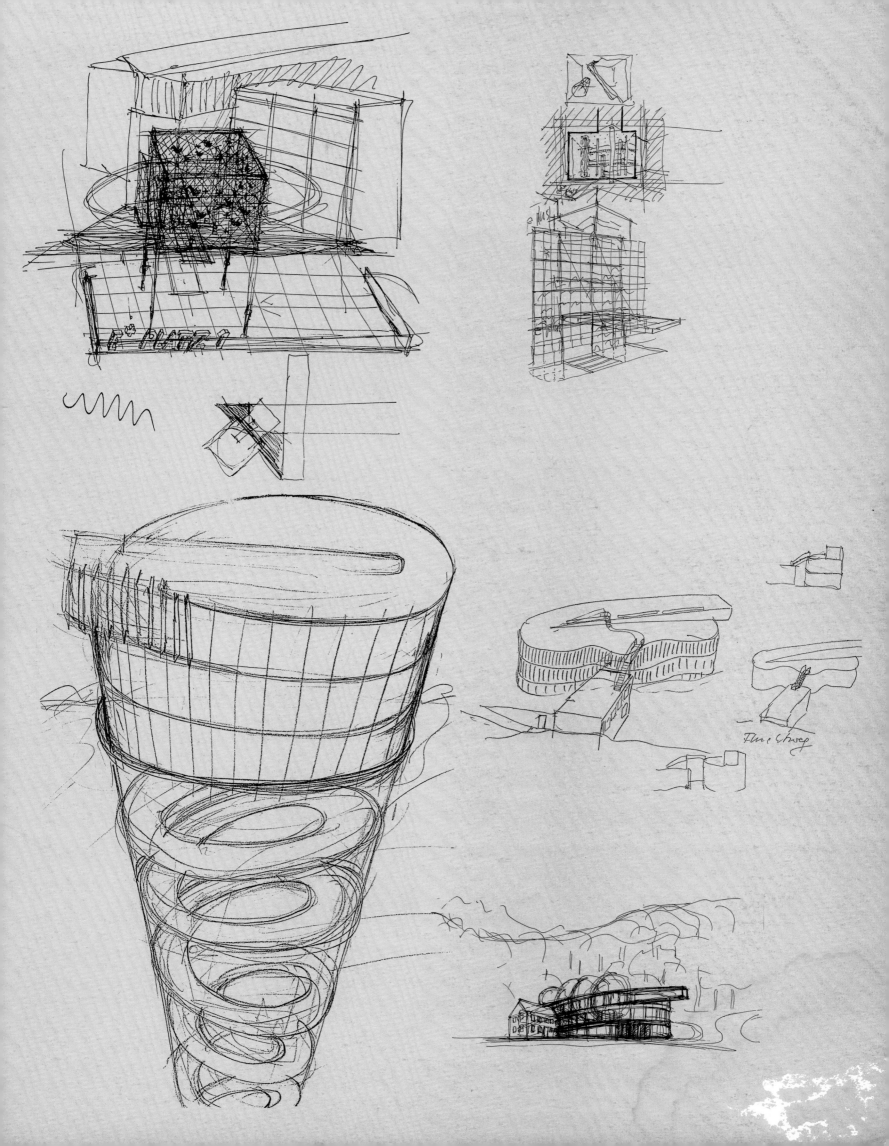

Blue Cubes and Reichling House

Ornamenta 1 – Built Fiction
Design for a Jewellery Exhibition, Pforzheim, 1989

... it is the reference principle that has to be doubted, this strategy by means of which they (the images) always appear to refer to a real world, to real objects, and to reproduce something which is logically and chronologically anterior to themselves. None of this is true. As simulacra, images precede the real to the extent that they invert the causal and logical order of the real and its reproduction.*

Jean Baudrillard

Ornamenta 1 questions the nature of the object. As Beatriz Colomina illustrated, since the beginning of the twentieth century we have been living in a time where the fixed place and the object in itself have been replaced by the period of relationships.

Zamp Kelp's design consists of a number of blue pilasters, 7.38m high, 1.4m deep and 1.2m wide, arranged symmetrically in response to the dimensions of the exhibition hall. The cubes establish a link between the inside of the building, and the garden and terrace outside . Each of the cubes inside has an opening on one side through which the viewer can see objects on display, seemingly suspended in an infinite space. The cubes situated outside have monitors installed in similar openings displaying images. Thus a dialogue between the physical nature of the object and its mediated image is established. By opposing the two different forms of appearance, Zamp Kelp illustrates a reality in which the distinction between object and image becomes problematic. Ornamenta 1 poses the question of the reference principle to the viewer without providing definite answers.

* Jean Baudrillard, *The Evil Demon of Images*,The Power Institute of Fine Arts, University of Sydney, 1978.

Blue Cube and Treasure Hill

Blue Cubes and Zamp Kelp

From Inside to Outside

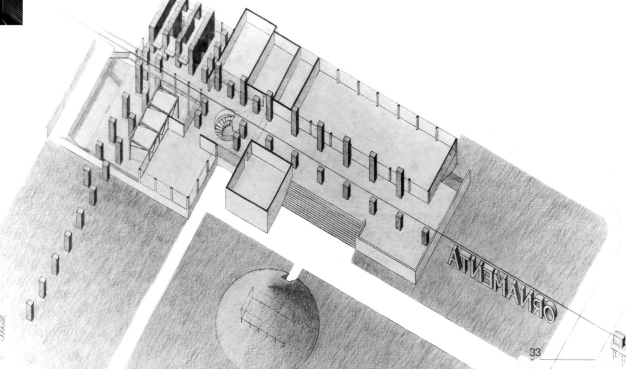

Isometric View of General Arrangement

Perspective Sketch of Central Massif

Central Massif

View of Courtyard

Forecourt with Panorama

Panorama Pavilion
Proposal for the Austrian Pavilion for the Seville Expo, 1989-90
(Zamp Kelp and D.S. Hoppe)

*Each surface is an interface between two environments that
is ruled by a constant activity in the form of an exchange
between the two substances placed in contact with each other.**

Paul Virilio

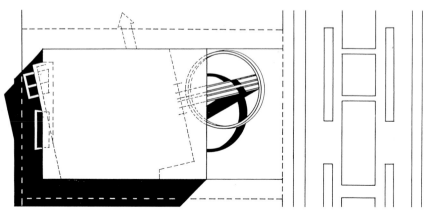

Siteplan

The pavilion's design is based on the assumption that two factors determine exhibition buildings: adaptability of space and the element of media. The latter is of significant importance, as it expresses the building's purpose to the outside world.

Zamp Kelp's proposal comprises two elements that relate to each other: the architectural structure and the square situated in front of it. The atmosphere and unmistakable identity of the square is determined by the circular structure hovering 8m above it, which serves as a carrier for media messages. The inside of the circular structure could, for instance, feature a panoramic image of the Alps, made from crystal glass, that one could experience by going up the escalator, penetrating the construction and reaching the entrance on the third floor. The skin of the building between exhibition space and square is transparent. A water curtain is situated on the side facing the square. The building is a steel-frame and glass structure which, in the relevant places, is fitted with a second layer for sun protection.

The use of the pavilion depends on location and event: whether it will serve as a container for rapidly changing contents or whether a specific use in combination with the building will create a unique identity. The temporal limits of the place's existence and its story are determined by its functional use.

* Paul Virilio, 'The Overexposed City', in Neil Leach, *Rethinking Architecture*, Routledge, London, 1997, p385.

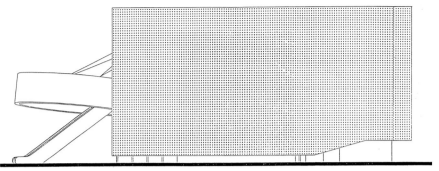

Side Elevation

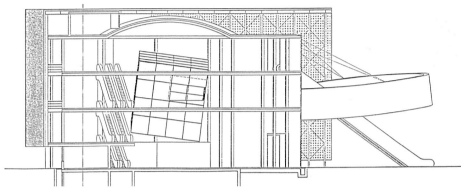

Section

Model Showing Interior; BELOW: Plan

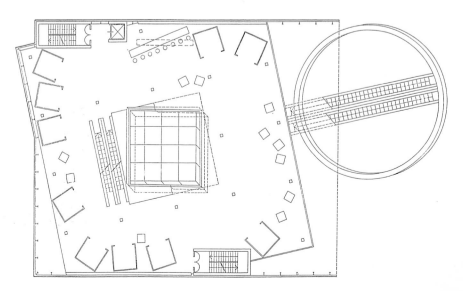

Night View

Exhibition Building with Panorama

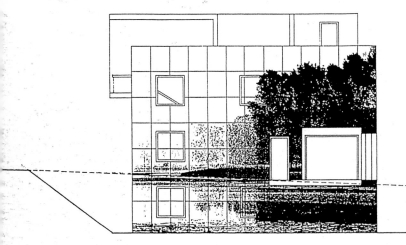 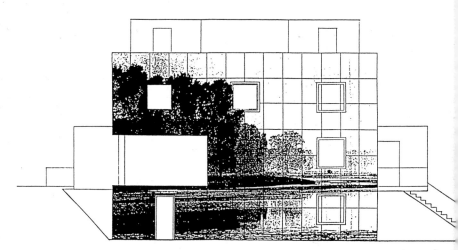

Facades; OPPOSITE: Model; Detail of Facade

House behind a River Landscape
Proposal for a Mixed-Use Building, Meerbusch, 1992

The surface of the city is the scaffolding for projection.*

Zamp Kelp

The projection and reality of the surrounding landscape determine the atmosphere of this house. In order to establish a relationship with the geographical conditions of the place, the chosen motif for the facade is a local river landscape. The penetration and layering of the facade with spatial elements is an attempt to visualise the conflict between the communication of information and the corporeality of daily experienced space.

Behind the facade, the building contains two main design elements: a load-bearing concrete frame and partition walls that can be arranged independently from the load-bearing structure. Thus the interior can be adapted according to the desired functions: it can be used either as a single house, a house / atelier or as flats.

In a time of unpredictable developments and changing circumstances, Zamp Kelp's design addresses the increased need for adaptability and flexibility.

*'Zamp Kelp in Conversation with Torsten Schmiedeknecht,' *Architectural Design*, Profile No 135, 9/10 1998, p45.

Building with Inserted Garage

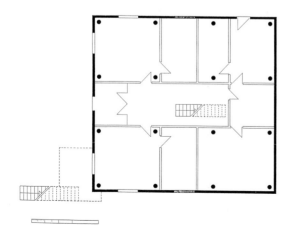

Basement

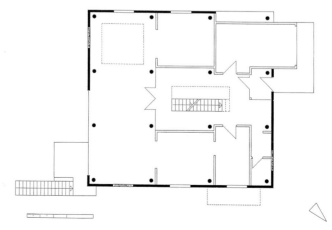

Ground Floor

View of Roof Terrace

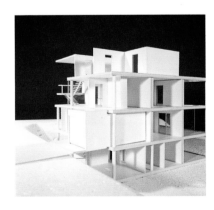

Model Showing Structure

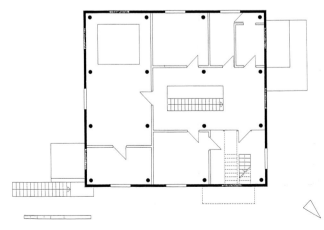

First floor

Ballroom with Retina

Water, Light, Vegetation
Permanent Installation in the Veterinary University Ballroom, Vienna, 1991-95

*Walls of light! Henceforth the idea of the window will be modified. Till now the function of the window was to provide light and air and to be looked through. Of these classified functions I should retain one only, that of being looked through.**

Le Corbusier

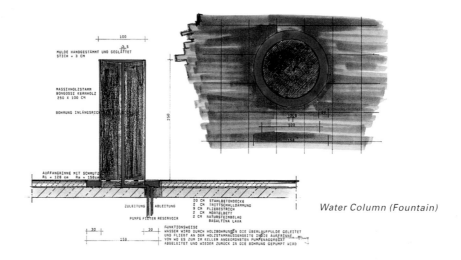

Water Column (Fountain)

Vegetation Object

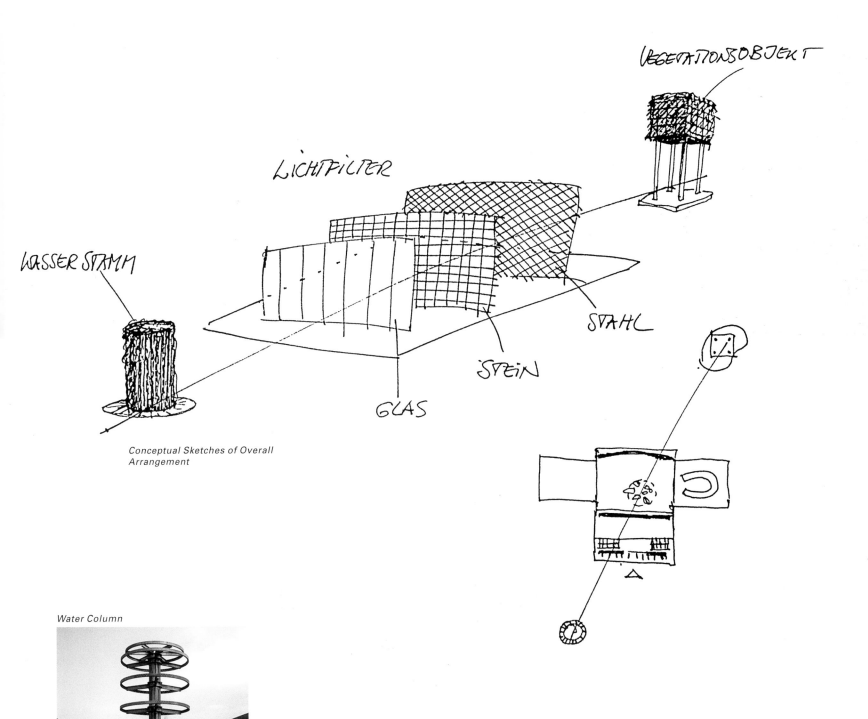

VEGETATIONSOBJEKT

LICHTFILTER

WASSER STAMM

STAHL

STEIN

GLAS

Conceptual Sketches of Overall Arrangement

Water Column

FROM ABOVE: Foyer with Glass Filter Wall;
Foyer with Estramos Wall

Water, light and vegetation, taken as the basis of all human and animal life, are the starting point for this project. The three elements – 'water trunk', 'light' and 'vegetation object' – are visualised along an axis running at an angle to the ballroom building's layout. 'Water trunk' is situated at one end of the axis, in front of the entrance to the ballroom. The opposite end of the axis is manifested by the 'vegetation object' set in the experimental garden in front of the main lecture theatre. 'Light', as the third element, occurs in three different conditions being filtered by three screens in the ballroom building. The filter wall in the foyer resembles a gate and features a white screen print of a cows liver, enlarged 4,400 times to cover 32 glass panels held in place by a steel space frame.

The 'estramos' wall at the entrance to the ballroom frames and stages the artificial light created behind it. The retina is a mobile 'paravant' in front of the windows of the ballroom. It consists of eight sliding stainless steel panels on to which the motif of the eye of an amphibian has been transferred by the means of perforations in different sizes.

The combination of light, image and symbol establishes an identity of place while it is questioning our understanding of physical space. By opposing the two installations 'water trunk' and 'vegetation object' with the display of different qualities of light the project plays with different architectural experiences. The objects can be seen as metaphors with tactile qualities, while the three screens are aimed at our visual perception. The transformation of objects, like the cow's liver, into large-scale images reveals the nature of objects' existence as one of relationships rather than 'object hood' itself. Simultaneously, a new identity is created in the form of the screens.

* Le Corbusier, *Twentieth Century Building and Twentieth Century Living*, p146.

Fiege Headquarters

*Competition Design for an Office and Administration Building,
Airport Münster-Osnabrück, 1997*

What is important to me is the topic, the theme of the project. Conveying the metaphor has become a central issue. I want the building to have an attitude and to take on a position regarding the brief.*

Zamp Kelp

Foyer Ground Floor; Perspective View

Foyer First Floor; Perspective View

Here, the main objective was a metaphorical translation of Fiege's corporate identity into a building, considering economic and ecological issues. The openness and dimensions of the site and its surroundings, and the client's wish to create views from the offices over the runways, determined the volumetric development of the headquarters.

Functionally, the project consists of two main elements: an artificial hill, containing a car park, and an eight-storey steel, glass and concrete slab of rhombic contours housing the office spaces.

The shape of the slab is derived from the Fiege logo, with the hexagonal form of the logo determining the basic articulation of the structural system. The offices accommodated in the slab face north and are accessed from the south. The building can be extended towards the south to provide central access. The north facade is layered, with a double-glazed inner layer and a single-glazed outer skin. The cavity in between houses the structure and serves as a buffer zone and a plenum for air extraction. In the summer, cold air flows through the cavity during the night to provide cooling. The south side of the building, which accommodates the circulation areas, consists of a thermally broken glazing system.

The building's immediate surroundings are modestly landscaped, featuring only the artificial hill and a lawn, at the centre of which shrubs are planted in the shape of the Fiege logo.

The location of the building at the airport raises an interesting issue: considering the railway as the cause for the beginning of the age of relationships between objects (as opposed to the existence of the object itself) and the beginning of the age of information, the airport can also be seen as a non-place, since it is more about the lines of connection between places than about the places themselves. Like the logo, the building is still an object in its own right, but one communicating information. The project is testing possibilities for establishing the identity of a non-location.

* 'Günter Zamp Kelp in Conversation with Torsten Schmiedeknecht', *Architectural Design*, Profile No 135, p144.

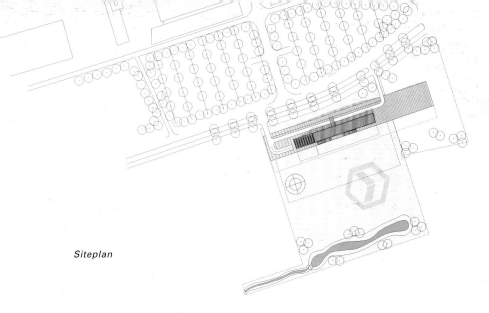

Siteplan

External Perspective View

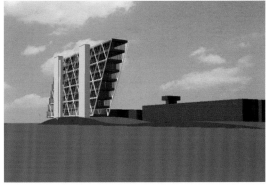

External Perspective View

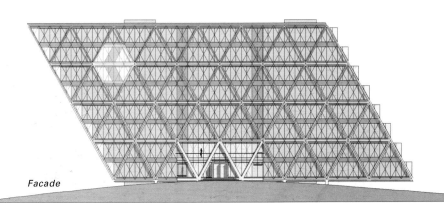

Facade

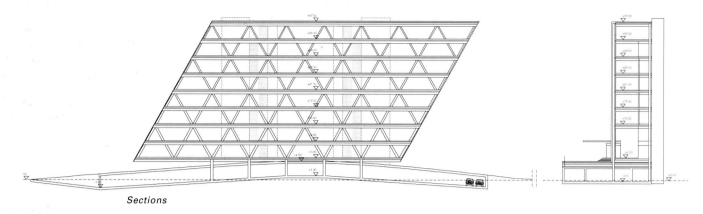

Sections

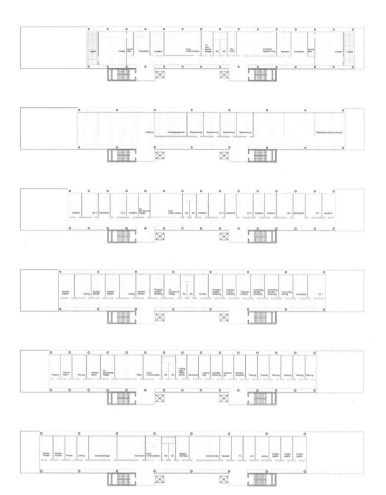

2nd-7th Floor Plans

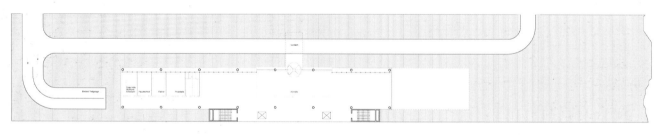

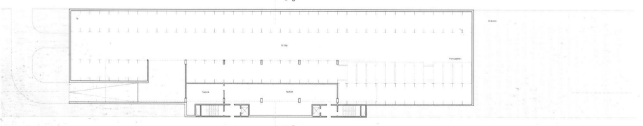

Ground Floor and Garage

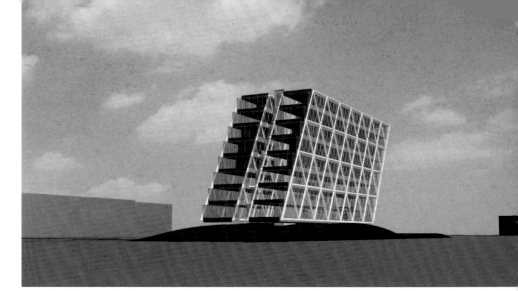

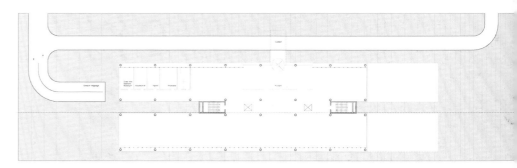

Perspective View and below Plan of Phase 2

View from 7th Floor

Millennium View

Park for the Cultural History of Stone, Steinbergen, 1997-2000

The craftsman travelling from place to place was communicative. On his way he acquired information and on his journey he passed it on through society. The pleasure of hiking, as in the still popular song, has also been attributed to the stones travelling along the beds of rivers, forced by the energy of water. One day, when the stones have left the realm of the waters, they will come to rest in the gravel pit, smooth, rounded and in large numbers. *

Zamp Kelp

Montage showing Zyklop

Zyklop under Construction

Interior of Tunnel Extension

Exterior of Tunnel Building

Exterior of Tunnel Building

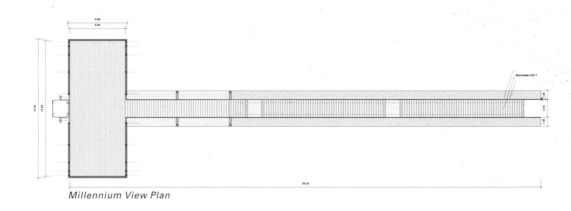

Millennium View Plan

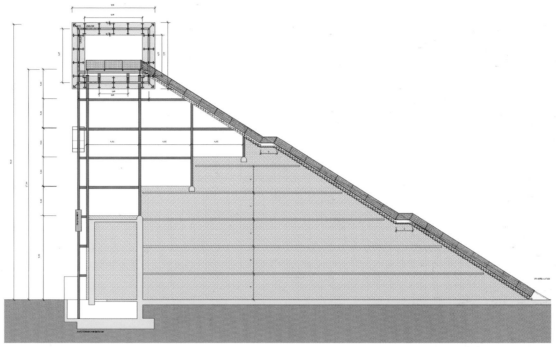

Millennium View Section

Over the course of history, man has extracted rocks from Schaumburg quarry in Steinbergen to use as a building material all over the world. In about 15 years, the quarry will be exhausted indeed large areas are already overgrown. Traces of the workings will serve as reminders of the place and as a starting point for the evolution of a physical, social space.

The project guides the visitor along a pathway that allows the history and nature of stone to be experienced in connection with our cultural history. It incorporates various installations such as Flock of Stones, Solar Forests and Stone School, in addition to a crater that symbolises the power of architectural intervention.

The pavilions are defined by green glass and stone walls, and have a narrative quality that enables different aspects of our cultural development to be suggested; for example, in House of Life, House of Time, House of Senses.

The climax is the Millennium View: a sculptural staircase construction on the ridge of the highest rock wall, which acts as a symbol for the whole site. Built from the quarry's stones, it terminates in a viewing platform set perpendicular to the direction of ascent. The cantilevered platform has a steel structure into which are integrated ten glass frames. Their parallel setting defines views across large areas of landscape to the north and south.

* Zamp Kelp, 'Die Steine selbst, so schwer sie sind?' in T Spiegelhalter, *Mediatecturen und Deponiekörper*, Häuser Verlag, Darmstadt, 1992, p36.

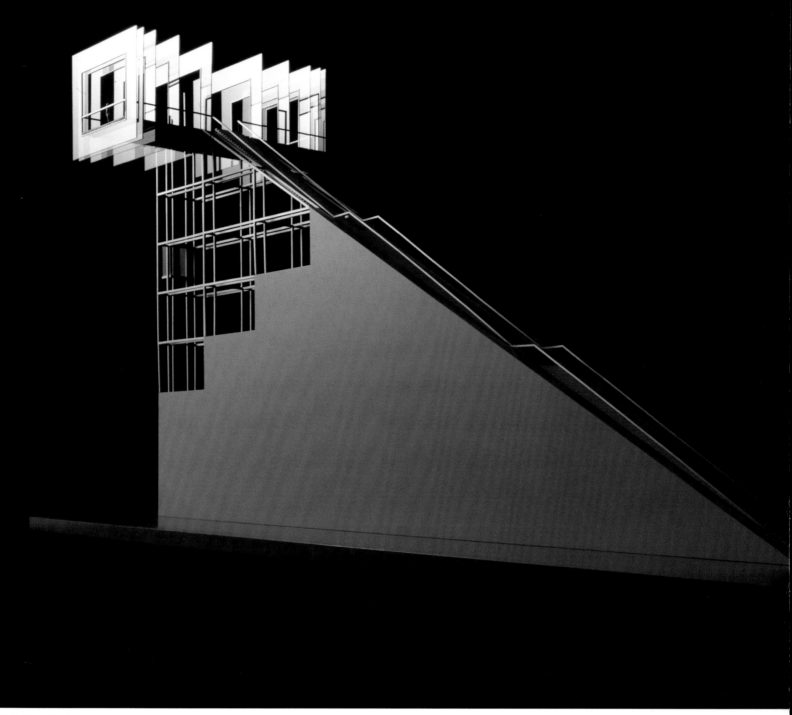

Night View Model

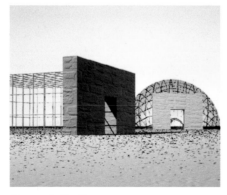

Stonegate Pavilion

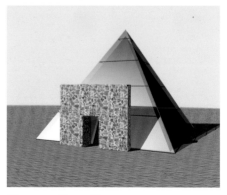

Stonegate Pyramid

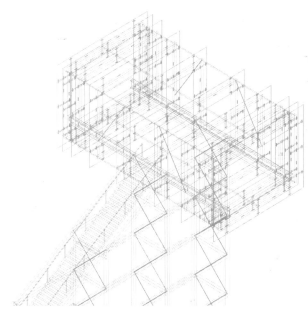

Viewing Platform

Stone Herd

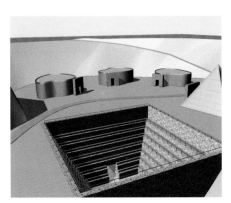

Arena

Space Henge

Beginning of Construction Work

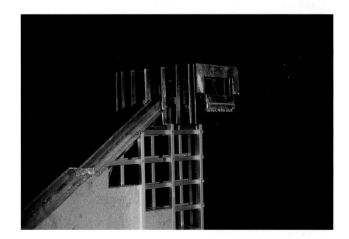

Photomontage of General Arrangement

FROM ABOVE: Wind Tunnel Model; OPPOSITE: Night View Model

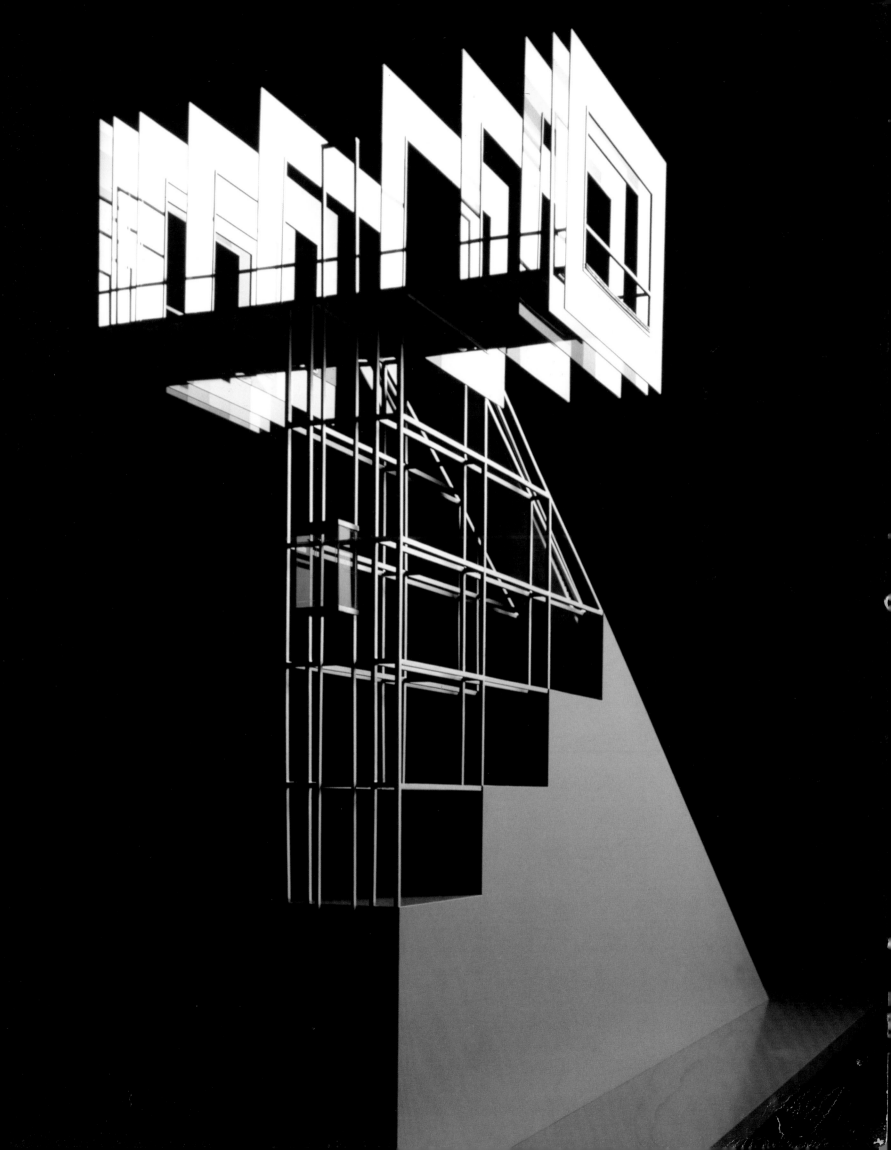

Perspective

Progress of Construction at 25.10.99

Perspective

Progress of Construction at 25.10.99

Progress of Construction at 25.10.99

Progress of Construction at 25.10.99

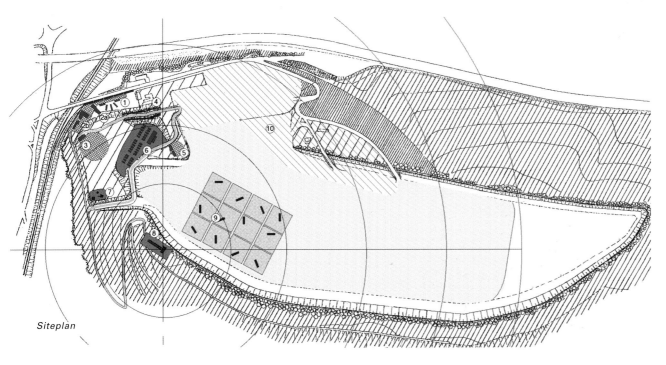

Siteplan

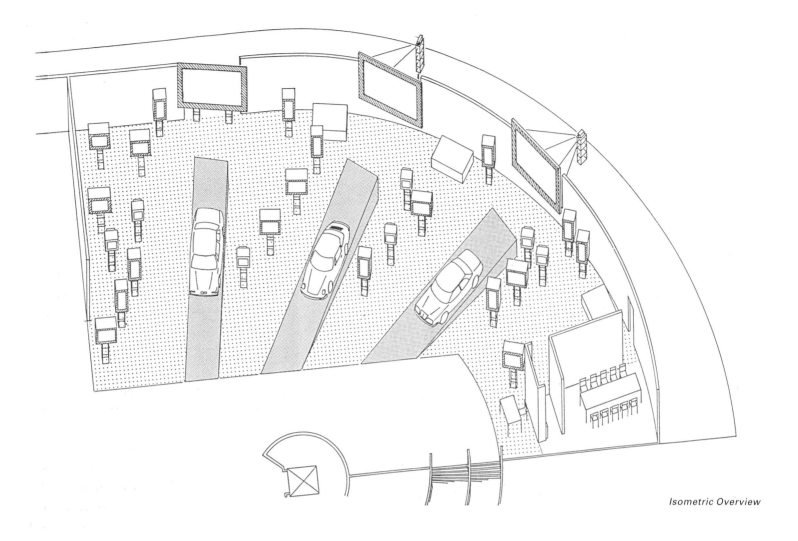

Isometric Overview

Visual Machines

Design for a Stand at the World Design Exposition, Nagoya, Japan, 1989

*An extended reality emerges that can be captured by the user because of the combination of physical and projected space. Thus the physical space gains a new importance as the stage for projections.** *

Zamp Kelp

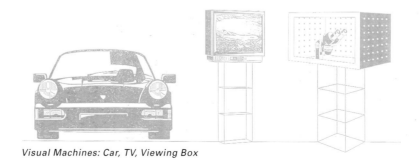

Visual Machines: Car, TV, Viewing Box

Views of Exhibition

Thoughts are subjective. Both intangible and invisible to others, they originate in our heads. An infinite number of ways of thinking from an infinite number of thinking machines. Thoughts have creative power. By projecting them into the reality of our living space we find our position in society. In order to visualise thoughts, we use model-descriptions in speech, writing or other means of representation, acoustically or in two or three dimensions. Thoughts need to be represented in order to make them understandable to others.

The projection of our thoughts into the world of physical realities is confronted with a reverse process, being perceived by our eyes, ears and organs of tactile perception.

The process of perception has become manifold and has thereby increased its speed. The same applies to the car – an experience machine – in which we experience landscape in a panoramic way through the course of our journey. At the same time, it applies to the sequences of the two-dimensional images of media projections on television. These images frequently dissolve and blur the boundaries between fiction and physical reality.

The German Design Exposition presents 'visual machines'. Car and TV monitor, the instruments of perception, are opposed by three-dimensional everyday objects. Through the classical vehicle of the raree show, selected design objects present themselves three-dimensionally as objects.[1] The overall effect is a comparison of the essential principles of present-day experience, and an overview and survey of up-to-date models of perception. The scenery of cars, monitors and raree shows is completed by the visitor's impression.

Notes

* 'Zamp Kelp in conversation with Torsten Schmiedeknecht', Düsseldorf, February 1999.

1 Baacke, Brandes, Erlhoff, *Design als Gegenstand*, Verlag Fröhlich & Kaufmann, Berlin, 1983.

Model

Drawing

House for the Styrian Autumn

Symbol and Accommodation for a Cultural Institute, Graz, 1990

To think about modern architecture must be to pass back and forth between the question of space and the question of representation ... it will be necessary to think of architecture as ... a series of overlapping systems of representations.*

Beatriz Colomina

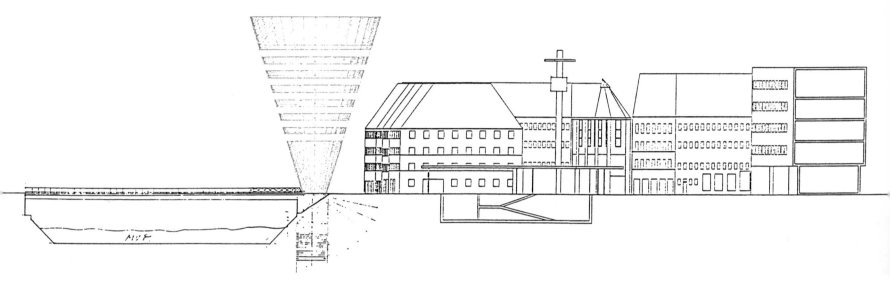

Elevation and Section Fischplatz

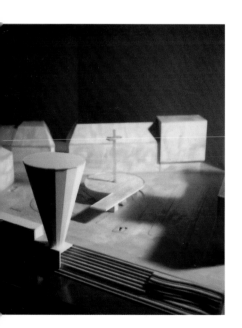

Every year the Styria region of Austria holds a cultural festival in its provincial capital, Graz. This is known as the Styrian Autumn and consists of two elements: the ephemeral element of the event itself and the permanent element of the festival's year-long administration and planning.

Within the coherent structure of Graz's old town, the Fischplatz is a place of disharmony. In an environment of listed buildings, it is a reminder of the multilayered normality of daily life. Half of it is a coach station, the other half a petrol station and beneath is an underground network of parking spaces. It is a place of functions and events, a place for the exchange of goods and people. Here, identity of place is the result of the superposition of urban activities. The design of the project is based on this superposition, regarding it as a source of vitality and attempting to make it legible.

Intensification is used as a strategic means of design, making the dense more dense and the lively more lively, by introducing an additional element. The project is concerned with the complexity of place and event. It articulates the aims of the cultural institution in a specific location and provides a presence for the festival in the city that goes beyond the temporal limits of the event.

The Styrian Autumn serves as a symbol for the city of Graz and has a reputation all over Europe. An upside-down cone represents all the activities linked to the Styrian Autumn and is a physical manifestation of the ambitions of the cultural institution.

* Beatriz Colomina, *Privacy and Publicity*, p13.

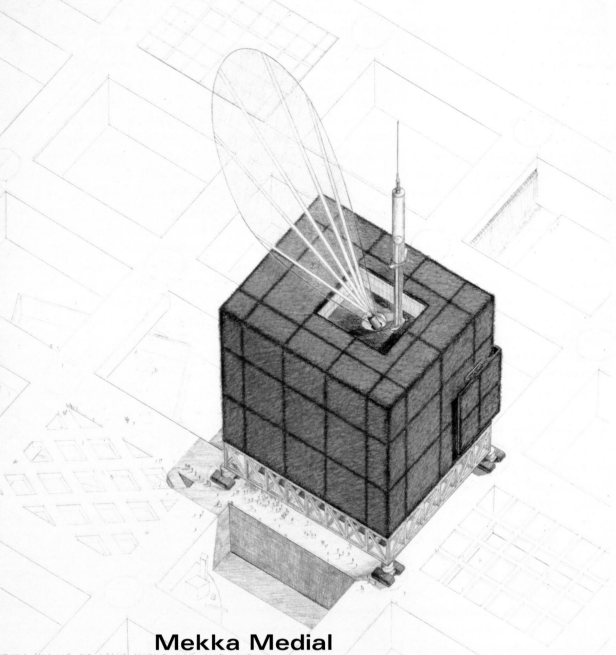

Mekka Medial
Project for City and Utopia Exhibition, Paris/Berlin, 1989–90

If the work of the city is the remaking or translating of man into a more suitable form than his nomadic ancestors achieved, then might not our current translation of our entire lives into the spiritual form of information seem to make of the entire globe, and of the human family, a single consciousness?*

Marshall McLuhan

Isometric View of Kaaba Mobile

Just as oriental Mecca is the religious and cultural centre of the Arab world, Mekka Medial is conceived as a centre for the observation and generation of cultural processes and perspectives in Europe. Religion is replaced with the study and application of media-technology, which often reaches religious dimensions in contemporary society.

Forty spaces, arranged in an order of eight by five and open to the sky, provide the areas for the creation and passing of different scenarios. A mobile cube can be moved over each of the 40 spaces, thus completing one scenario at a time. The cube itself consists of a central space that is surrounded by accommodation for administration, workshops and broadcasting studios. Like a queen bee, looking after her honeycombs, the Kaaba Mobile nurtures the 40 'stages'.

Identity is created via the event. Architecture, providing the space for these events, is thus part of the identity. An integrated TV channel broadcasts the activities taking place in Mekka Medial and enables people all over Europe to participate.

The project attempts to illustrate the link between the production of mediated images and projections, and the place of their production. In the age of non-places and non-identities, Mekka Medial emphasises the importance of physical place and space by providing the possibility for 'pilgrimage' to it for people to take part in a permanent communicative event. A reality consisting of the combination of corporeal and virtual elements is being created.

* Marshall McLuhan, *Understanding Media*, p61.

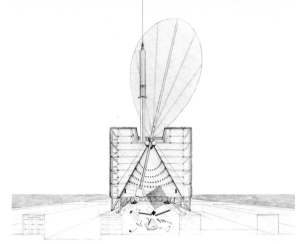

Section

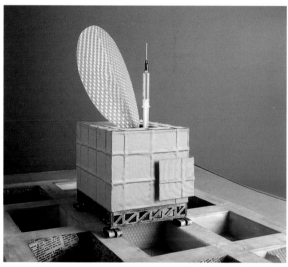

Model

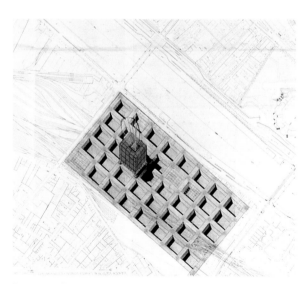

Isometric Overview; BELOW: Model

View from North West

Neanderthal Museum

Museum for the History of Mankind, Mettman, 1993–96
(Zamp Kelp and J.Krauss and A.Brandhuber)

[The] central feature of the building is a spiral ramp serving the different exhibition spaces determining the museum's appearance. Through the ribbon like ramp, synonymous with infinity, the building becomes a spatial parable for the evolution of man that is also part of infinity. *

Zamp Kelp

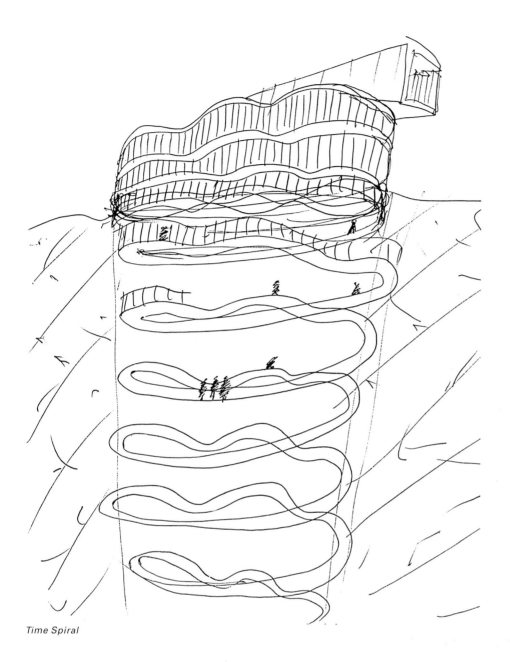

Time Spiral

Cover (M.C.Escher)

Abstraction for me is an important means, maybe the only possible chance to allow us to become aware of different aspects and to enable us to project ourselves.[1]

Zamp Kelp

The Neanderthal Museum was completed in October 1996, designed in collaboration with Julius Krauss and Arno Brandlhuber. It lies not far from Düsseldorf, in the Neander Valley, named after the remains of the skeleton that was found there in a cave in 1856. The project is a fine example of how the means of abstraction can be employed in conjunction with a metaphorical interpretation of a brief to create a unique sense of identity and place.

Whether one reads into the building's alien appearance the character of the cave, employs the spiral as a symbol for the development of man, sees it as a metaphor for the valley itself or prefers to allocate some similarities to an amoeba (probably not coincidentally the Greek word for change), it is impossible to categorise the building with a standard description or to place it within a common typology.

The Neanderthal itself is a typical recreational tourist area and the new building is situated next to the customary bars and hotels that employ the language

West Elevation

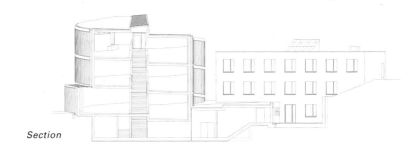

Section

View of Interior with Lift

of vernacular architecture. These tourist venues proclaim the eternally present *Gemütlichkeit* that foreign tourists seem so keen to find in Germany. (There is even a Neanderthal man on display in a cave in one of the restaurant venues.) The contrast between the two kinds of architecture and display could not be greater. While encountering a *'Venturiesque'* environment of applied signs that have become architecture but failed to distinguish the Neanderthal from any other *'natural'* tourist site, the new museum allows the place to recreate its own story through the sophisticated application of form and material.

The story the building communicates is one of change and development. It is the story of infinity and tells of the freedom of interpretation, communicated both on a direct level – through the possibility of multiple readings of its material nature – and also on a metaphorical level, through the architect's choice of materials and method of spatial arrangement. The museum with it's strange green glass skin, reflecting and absorbing light at the same time, operates at the fringe between the realms of physical and projectional space.

In contrast to the initial competition design, in which the spiral was planned as a narrow passage surrounding three towers (therefore allowing the visitor to choose which route to take), the spiral as built is a broad ramp that accommodates the exhibition. It leads the visitor to the viewing platform that overlooks the valley, offering what Zamp Kelp has called a view into uncertainty.

The spiral arrangement encourages the visitor constantly to make non-chronological cross references; by looking across the central staircase to the ascent or

Central Staircase;
OPPOSITE: North Elevation

View from South

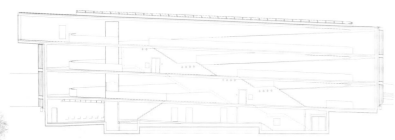

Section

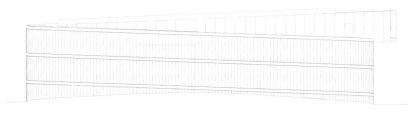

North Elevation

Entrance

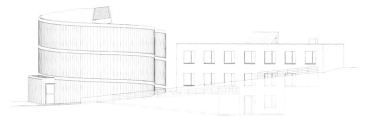

East Elevation

Interior

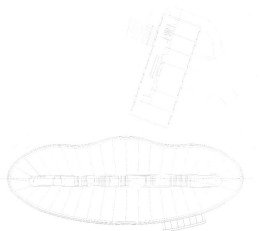

First Floor and Ground Floor

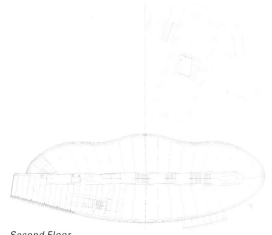

Second Floor

Aerial View

descent opposite, an individual pattern of man's history can be constructed by forging new links with the present and future. Such impressions are not unlike ideas expressed in the work of artists such as Dan Graham or Gordon Matta-Clarke, and explained by Walter Benjamin in 1937:

Historicism presents an eternal image of the past, historical materialism a specific and unique engagement with it ... The task of historical materialism is to set to work an engagement with history original to every new present. It has recourse to a consciousness of the present that shatters the continuum of history.[2]

According to Zamp Kelp, the Neanderthal Museum acts as a means of providing a better understanding of the world and offers an open interpretation of the past, present and future. This leaves room for curious speculations and discoveries, and does not leave the contemporary model of the development of society unquestioned. Most interesting in these respects is the fact that there remains a controversial debate about the taxonomic classification of the Neanderthals, having been classed both as a separate species: *Homo neanderthalensis*, and, alternatively, as a subspecies of *Homo sapiens*.

Notes

* Zamp Kelp, text for competition entry for the Neanderthal Museum, 1994.

1 'Zamp Kelp in Conversation with Torsten Schmiedeknecht', *Architectural Design*, Profile No 135, p45.

2 Walter Benjamin, 'Eduard Fuchs, Collector and Historian' (1937), in *One-Way Street and Other Writings*, trans Kingsley Shorter, New Left Books, London, 1979, p352.

Building and Urban Situation

Georg Schäfer Museum
Competition Design for an Art Gallery, Schweinfurt, 1997

The problematic nature of the border appears not only at the inner edge, between frame and picture, but also at the outer edge, between frame and world. *

Annette Michelson

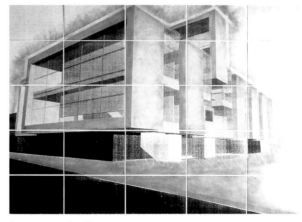

Entrance to the City

Conceptual Sketches

The frame as mediator between two-dimensional representations and the surroundings in which they are displayed is used as a tool, both in the visual sense and in the sense of spatial organisation, in the project for the Museum Georg Schäfer. The collection to be displayed consists of approximately 300 nineteenth-century German paintings.

Zamp Kelp's design seeks to explore the possibilities of framing. A series of 13 frames, arranged one behind the other, builds the structural framework of the museum. While being a container for the collection of paintings, the building also establishes an identity within the urban fabric by directly employing the frame as a metaphor. The question that arises for the visitor is: What is being framed? The outside world is being put on display from the inside via the frames. The inside is being framed from the outside. The visitor becomes part of the exhibition by being an element in the succession of framed images and objects: painting – frame – visitor – frame – outside world. Thus the relationship between work of art and visitor is being questioned, and a dialogue is allowed to take place. Despite its formal rigidity, the project is part of a tradition of work by artists such as Seurat, Mondrian and, most of all, Frank Stella, all of whom have addressed the issue of the frame. Both Stella and Zamp Kelp accept the museum as an institution but offer new ways of interpreting its spatial concept and thus the display of works of art.

* Annette Michelson, 'Frameworks' in Robert Morris, *The Mind/Body Problem*, exhibition catalogue, The Solomon R Guggenheim Foundation, New York, 1994, p55.

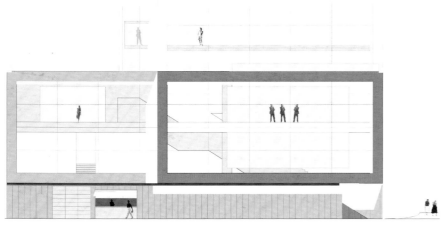

South Elevation

Perspective View from South

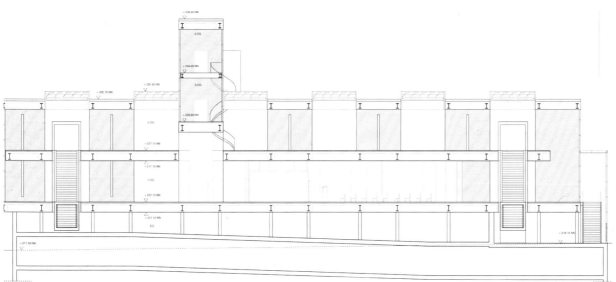

Long Section

Interior Space

Entrance Perspective View

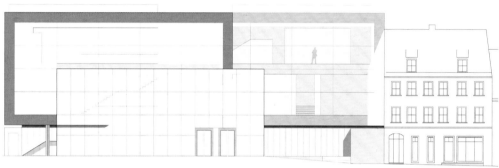

North Elevation Entrance

Interior

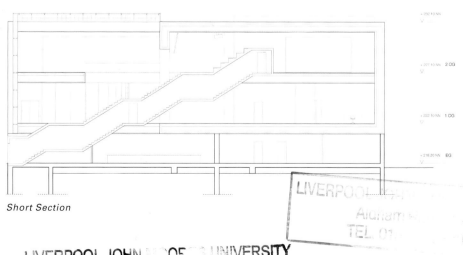

Short Section

Model

Archaeological Museum
Competition Design, Herne, 1997

Memory Becomes the Conscience of the City.*

Aldo Rossi

Perspective View of Entrance

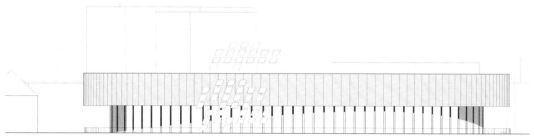

South Facade

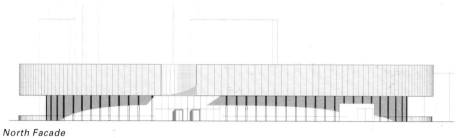

North Facade

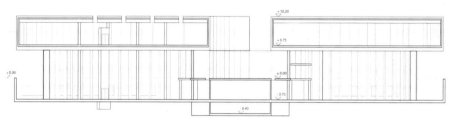

Section

The key to archaeology lies beneath the surface of the earth, either invisible or communicated by codes. An archaeological museum is a place were the hidden past is revealed in a direct or metaphorical way. As well as being a place for scientific research, it houses objects from the history of mankind, and its task is to stage these objects in a coherent and comprehensible way. Zamp Kelp's design for the archaeological museum in Herne attempts to make the building a parable for its contents.

First, the building's identity is established in its urban environment. A rectangle, approximately describing the area of the site, provides the base for the intervention. Out of this base, an elliptical slab (2,400m², 6.5m high) is cut out and raised to a height of 12m. This device metaphorically translates the theme of archaeological excavation, creating the cover for the archaeological trench that circumscribes the lower part of the exhibition building. The trench, providing the space for archaeological scenarios, is open to visitors. It also serves as a light source for the subterranean service areas. The roof of the raised slab is an accessible terrace, accommodating a 'forest' of solar panels and providing visitors with views over the urban context.

Functionally, the building is divided into two main exhibition spaces: the area for the permanent exhibition that is situated within the volume of the raised slab

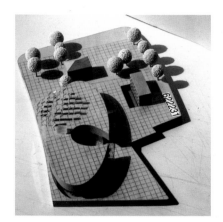

Model

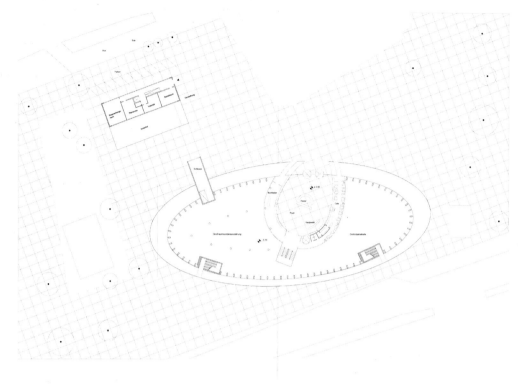

Ground Floor Plan

on the first floor and the double-height space for large objects and special exhibitions on the lower ground floor.

The surfaces of the roof terrace and the square, in accordance with the concept of the cut, are identically conceived as concrete or stone pavers. The cuts of the elliptical slab and the archaeological ditch are both clad in ceramic tiles.

It was kind of the thin edge of what was being seen that interested me as much, if not more than, the views that were being created. The layering, the strata, the different things that are being severed provided the simplest way to create complexity.[1]

The concept of the cut does not only metaphorically translate the theme of the project, it also offers a variety of spaces to be experienced in the urban context. The roof terrace offers the possibility to locate oneself within the immediate surroundings and the city. The enclosure of the first-floor exhibition space plays with the idea of the cave and isolates the exhibited objects from the context, offering views only into the elliptic cut out over the entrance area. The lower-ground-floor level connects the building to the site. Being surrounded by the archaeological trench, it illustrates the dual relationship between the act of excavation and the traces that are left from it, thus creating a new identity of the place.

Notes

* Aldo Rossi, quoted in Brian Wallis, 'Dan Graham's History Lessons' in *Rock my Religion*, pxv.
1 Liza Bear, 'Gordon Matta-Clark: Splitting (The Humphrey Street building)', *Avalanche*, no 10, December 1974.

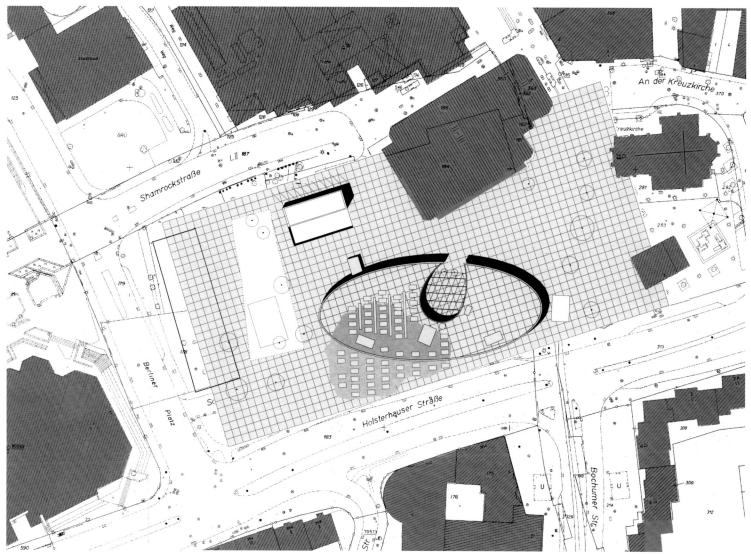

Siteplan

Interior Perspective

Archeological Trench

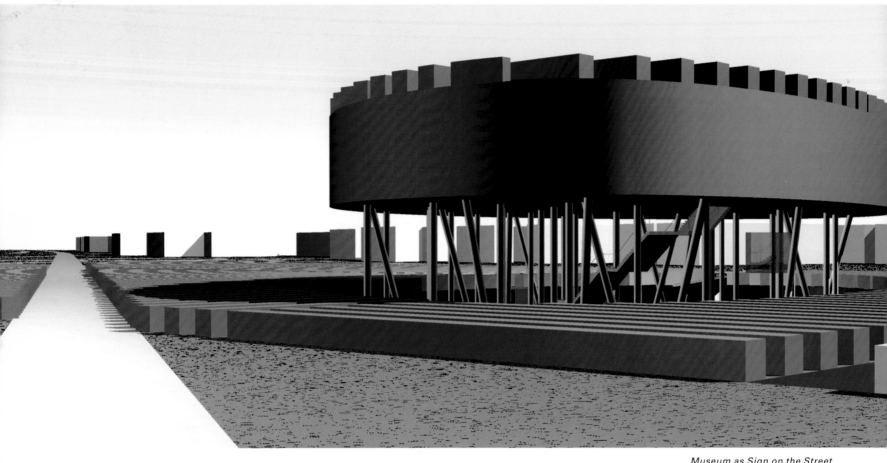

Museum as Sign on the Street

International Art Museum

Competition Design for a Centre for Nature, Art, Local History and Information, Lanzarote, 1999

This project strikes me as a combination of two different genres. One is: I am an architect and I am interested in conceptual art. The other is: I am an architect and I'm interested in the relationship between stories and myth and identity, and I need to represent that in some kind of monument. Both things happen at the same time.*

Paul Davies

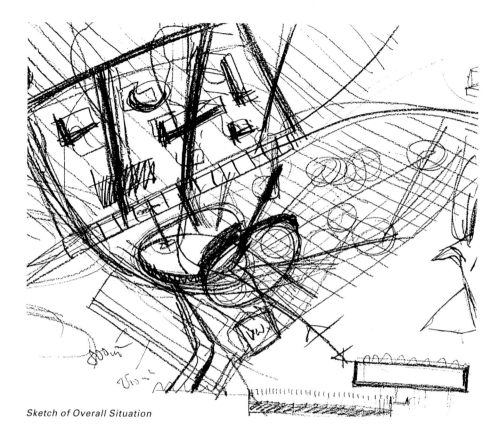

Sketch of Overall Situation

Due to the effects of tourism there has been a change in Lanzarote's population structure in the last few years. The island's future development will be determined by the refusal of unrestricted expansion. Instead, the focus will be on a different kind of tourism, one that respects and incorporates the island's natural structure. The name Lanzarote will become synonymous with ecological sustainability.

This change of focus, or identity, can be represented by the means of a landmark or symbol on the island. In Zamp Kelp's design, the broken lance as a sign becomes a metaphor for the name Lanzarote. A huge, dejected lance-tip more than 80m high and built from steel becomes the symbol for change. A cable car brings people up to the lance's tip, offering views over the coastline, the ocean and Arrecife.

The museum itself comprises a centre for nature, art, local history and information, to be housed in sixteen rooms of an existing subterranean cistern. The spatial concept employs two main strategies: first, the cistern's plan is mirrored along its side, leaving a space 5m wide and 120m long between existing and mirrored space; second, an area of 3,000m² is metaphorically 'punched out' of the island and raised 8m above ground level. Supported on a fragile column structure, this piece of floating island will be visible for miles around. Below it, in the negative space created, is a shaded square located on the same level as the cistern.

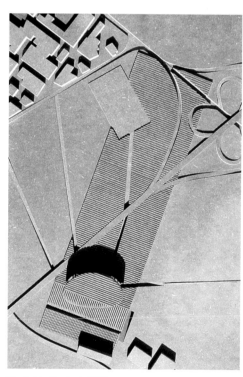

Model in Scale 1:1000

The floating island's external appearance is determined by the use of Lanzarote's typical local lava stone and only the roof is planted with cacti. The sunken square's surface treatment is like that of the floating island: only the floodable central area

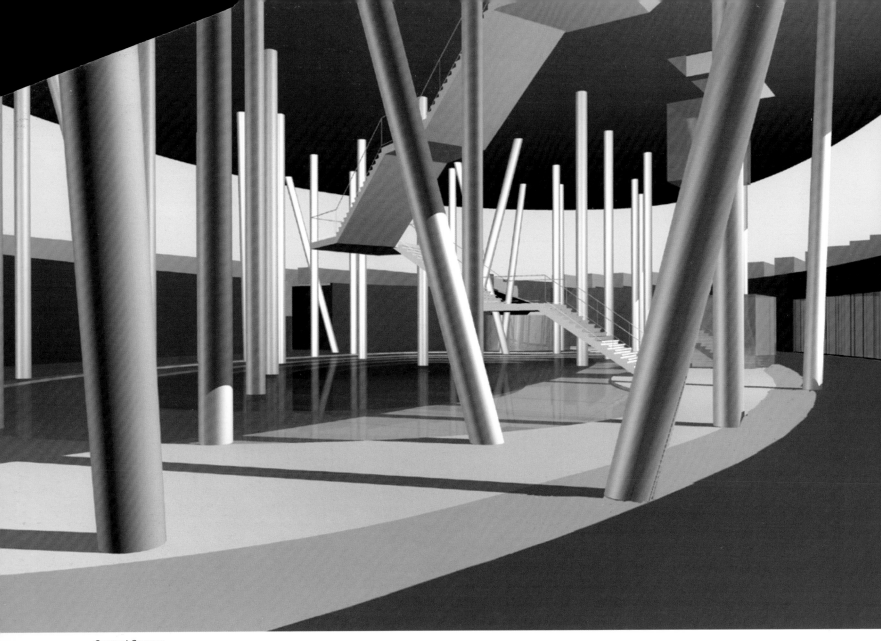

Central Square

is kept white, along with the timber columns supporting the Centre for Art and History, in reference to Cesar Manriquez.

The roof of the former cistern is covered with photovoltaic panels, signalling its new content. The energy generated from these panels is used to illuminate the newly planted cacti field, shining cochineal red by night.

The museum, with its floating piece of island at the Maretas, stands for a new era of sustainable development in Lanzarote's near future. The Lanza Rota as a symbol for the island's identity stands diametrically opposed to the museum. In between is located the centre of Arrecife. The street of Art and Media links these two poles and offers a series of permanent and temporary activities, enhancing the urbanity of Arrecife and redetermining the island's profile.

* Paul Davies in conversation with Torsten Schmiedeknecht, South Bank University, London, 3 June 1999.

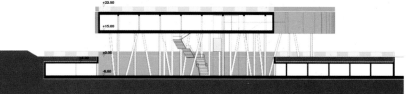

Section

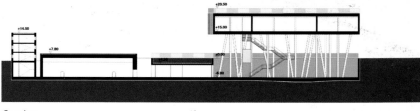

Section

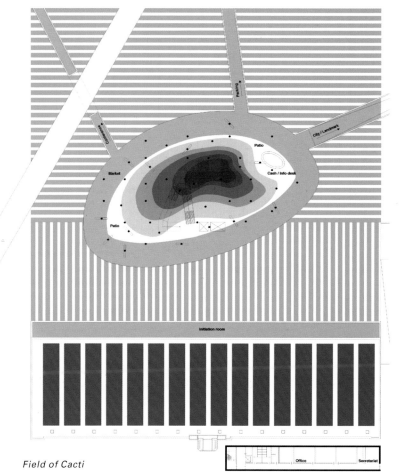

Field of Cacti

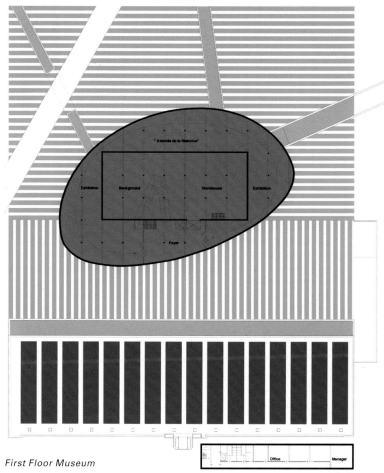

First Floor Museum

Lower Ground Floor Museum in
Existing Cistern

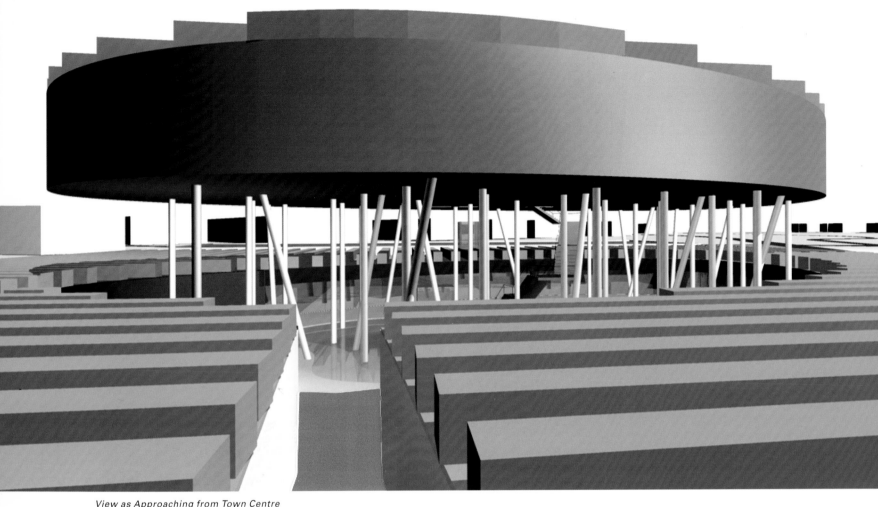

View as Approaching from Town Centre

Lanza Rota

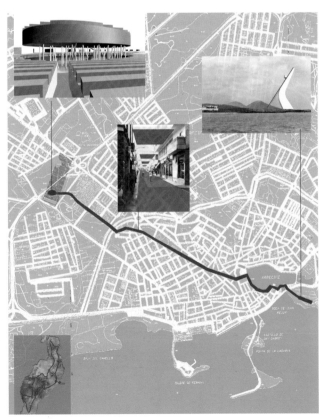

Street of Art and Media

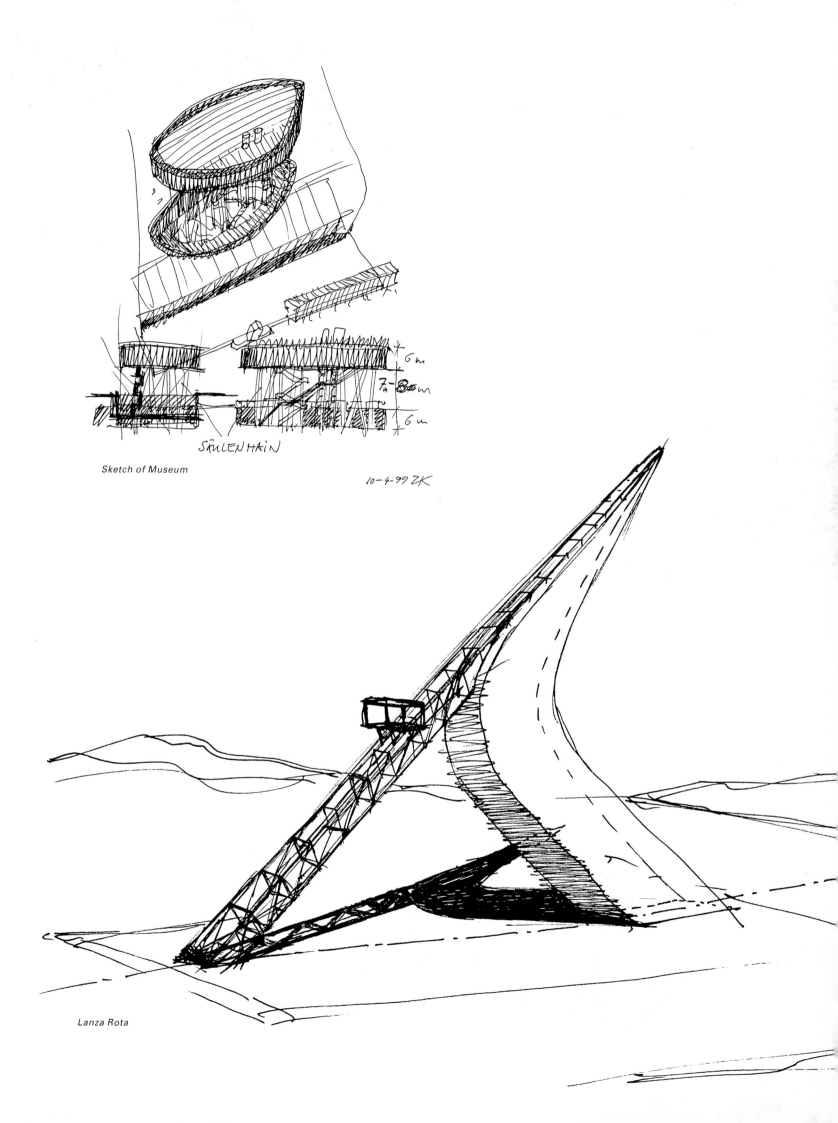

SÄULENHAIN

Sketch of Museum

10-4-99 ZK

Lanza Rota

Model

Transformation
Proposal for a Building on a Bunker, Cologne, 1990

*Historical memory is a web that is woven through the pub-
lic experience of the city, the forms of popular culture, and
the routines of everyday life.**

Brian Wallis

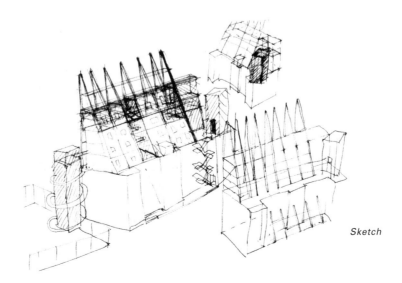

Sketch

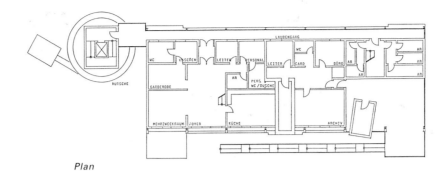

Plan

Roof Plan

SPIELPLATZ

KÖRNERSTRASSE

As the place where the persecution of the Jewish people reached its most terrifying dimension, the site in Körnerstraße is one of historical importance and meaning. Still, it would be questionable to focus exclusively on the site's problematic history without making reference to the normality of daily life taking place in its surroundings. In Transformation, the place surrenders its camouflage and appears as a strong element in its urban context. The complex relationship of the site's unforgettable past and its new contents that relate to present and future creates an atmosphere of energy. The central conceptual element is an accessible blue box (5m x 3.2m x 10.7m) containing Felix Droese's piece *Ich habe Anne Frank umgebracht* (I have killed Anne Frank).

The two lower levels inside the bunker contain multifunctional spaces for cultural events. The upper level is reserved for the archive of a planned centre of documentation. The new structure on top of the bunker contains the archive's administration, an international kindergarten and living spaces. The top floor is a light and airy exhibition-event-action space contextually relating to the multifunctional spaces in the bunker. A viewing platform at the height of 30m provides a vantage point over Cologne, placing Transformation in the context of the city.

* Brian Wallis, 'Dan Graham's History Lessons' in *Rock My Religion*, pxvi.

Model

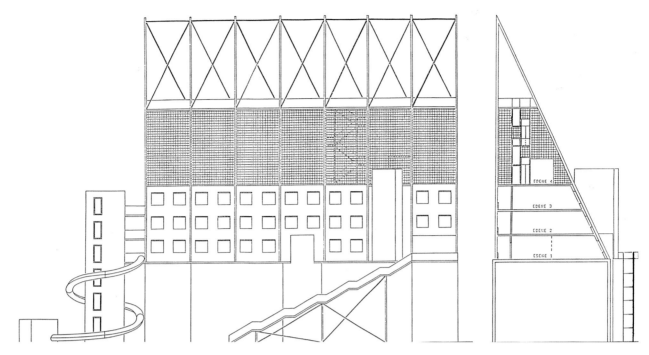

Elevation, Section

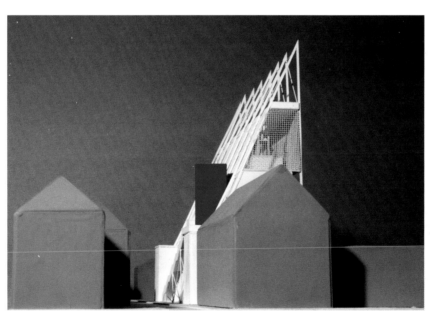

Street Situation

Close-up View of Completed Building

Expanding Space

Completion of an Existing Group of Buildings, Meinerzhagen, 1992
(Zamp Kelp and Christoph Kessler)

Everything exists by virtue of its limits. *
Robert Musil

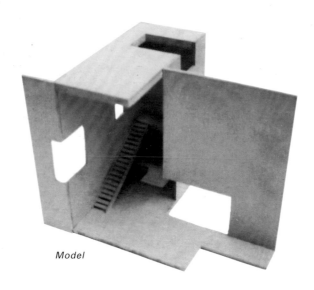

Model

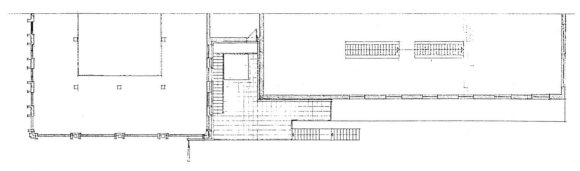

Plan

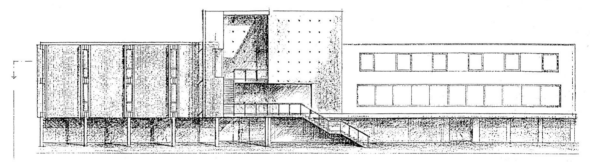

Elevation

External View

The project mediates between two existing buildings that both provide accommodation for a furniture showroom. The new element, while being an external space, articulates itself with the characteristics of an interior space. By expressing the relationship between inside and outside, Zamp Kelp explores the nature of boundary and threshold. The blue colour of the mediating building at first seems to establish a clear boundary, but the complexity of the volume reveals the single elements of the composition. The surfaces take on different appearances depending on the angle from which they are viewed. Slabs become angles; volumes become surfaces, and vice versa. Thus each element plays a multiple role. Outside wall of the existing surface or inside of the new? The notion of limit and boundary is readdressed every time one moves. What remains constant is the colour blue, providing the place with an overall identity, within which the identities of the parts are in a state of flux.

* Robert Musil, *Der Mann ohne Eigenschaften*, Rowohlt, Hamburg.

Green Glass Surface

Design for the Entrance of E Plus Mobilfunk Headquarters, Düsseldorf, 1995-96

During long periods of history, the mode of human sense perception changes with humanity's entire mode of existence. The manner in which human sense perception is organised, the medium in which it is accomplished, is determined not only by nature but by historical circumstance. *

Walter Benjamin

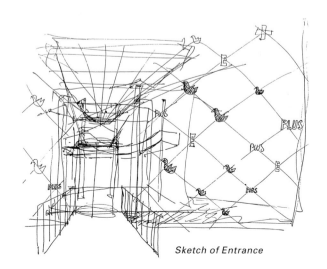

Sketch of Entrance

Facade Facing Forecourt

Side View of Completed Scheme

The design of the forecourt establishes the existing headquarters in its immediate environment. The main feature of the design is a green glass wall, 16m high and 20m wide, that is supported by a steel space frame on to which the image of a flock of birds has been transferred, signifying the E-Plus logo. The glass wall is penetrated by a cantilevered canopy underneath which one enters the foyer that is located behind the wall in a 10m-high glass cube. Internally, the cube is structured by two galleries and its three storeys relate to each other by means of a map of the world that is situated on the back wall stretching the cube's full height. The map is horizontally structured into time-zones, thus illustrating the context of place, time and communication as the realm in which E-Plus is operating.

Düsseldorf is clearly marked on the map, signifying its position in the global context, while the forecourt, glass wall and information desk create a strong identity for E-Plus within the immediate surroundings of the city.

* Walter Benjamin, 'The Work of Art in the Age of Mechanical Reproduction', in *Illuminations*, Fontana Press, London, 1973; reprinted 1992, p216.

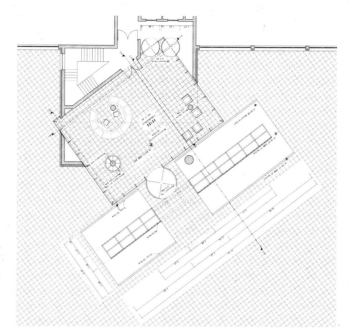

Siteplan

Green Glass

Empty Space

Zero-Gravity Space

Project to Alter an Aldo van Eyck Building, Düsseldorf, 1998-99

To visualise geographically the multitude of sociological events regarding their time-space relationship will be one of architecture's new tasks. Cityscape becomes legible at its surfaces. This is where architecture has the chance to react to changes in the biological and geometrical space. The architectural skin or surface has been detached from the architectural construction. The surface has become an independent and flexible medium in the urban landscape. Via the architectural surface the attempt is being made to establish a new relationship between the new and the old parts of public space.*

Zamp Kelp

This design is for the conversion of the former driveway of the Schmela Gallery in the centre of Düsseldorf. Built for the gallery owner Alfred Schmela, and opened with a show of work by the German Fluxus artist Joseph Beuys in 1971, the building represents the only work executed by Aldo van Eyck in Germany. It now provides an interesting opportunity to look at the theories of both Aldo van Eyck and Zamp Kelp, and the way in which their writings have been articulated in their projects and buildings. Van Eyck said in his statement for the 1959 Otterlo Congress that:

Man is always and everywhere essentially the same. He has the same mental equipment though he uses it differently according to his cultural or social background Modern architects have been harping continually on what is different in our time that even they have lost touch with what is not different, with what is always essentially the same. [1]

Nineteen years later Zamp Kelp wrote:

At the end of the twentieth century we are becoming nomads again, but nomads in an inverted sense. Without having to relocate ourselves, we experience the projected world that is drifting by. Our therefore altered sense of perception will have an impact on architecture. The often discussed farewell from the mechanised world also means a good-bye to clear and definitive contexts. Thus the role of architecture as geometrical space is about to change. Architecture has over the years given away elements of its traditional tasks. [2]

Van Eyck's concern with the threshold is clearly illustrated in the design of the gallery. It is a concern that emphasises the relevance of an outside and an inside in architectural space, and therefore supports the idea that there can be an authentic structure and construction which could in turn create a sense of place. Van Eyck was aware of the changes in modern society but took a different approach to that postulated by Zamp Kelp today. He blamed modern architecture for the 'eradication of both style and place'[3] and Kenneth Frampton writes in his *Critical History of Modern Architecture:*[4]

His [van Eyck's] doubts as to the ability of the profession to meet the pluralistic demands of society, without the mediation of a vernacular, led him to question the authenticity of the society itself. In 1966 he asked: 'If society has no form – how can architects build its counter form? [5]

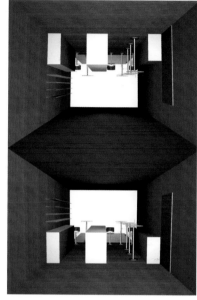

Conceptual Visualisation

Evening View

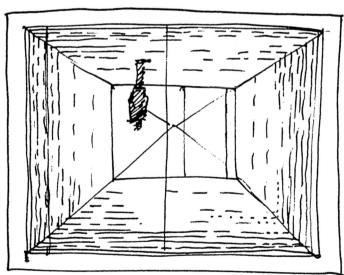

Sketch

Frontal View from Courtyard

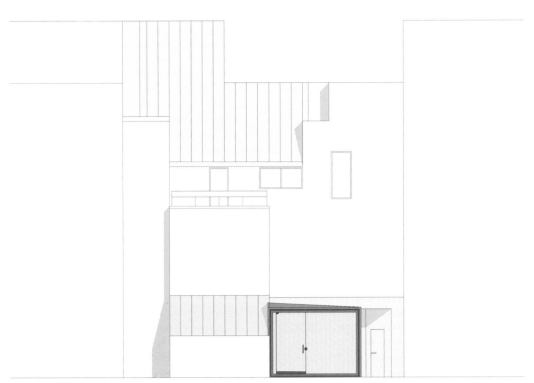

Courtyard Elevation

Side View from Courtyard

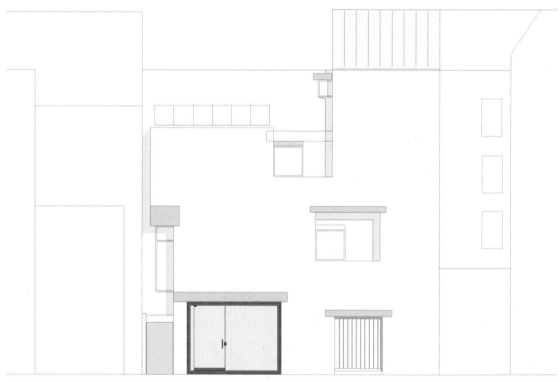

Street Elevation

Courtyard Elevation

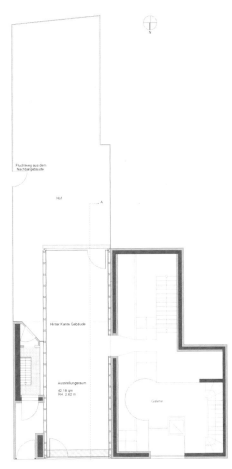

Plan Showing Inserted Space

Street Elevation

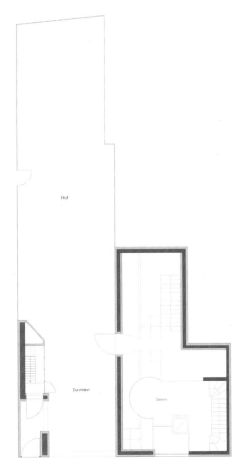

Plan Before Alteration

Symptomatic of his positive approach to the question of authenticity in society, Zamp Kelp wrote in 1996:

Built fictions in the physical space are opposed by dematerialised monuments in the virtual part of our perception. Space as experience cannot be thought of without virtual elements any longer. Vice versa the relationship between the virtual world and the physical world becomes an essential for our perception of society.[6]
The importance of surface as an independent medium and a tool for Zamp Kelp to generate space, both in the corporeal and in the virtual sense, becomes evident in Zero-Gravity Space. Apart from the two glazed end facades, the interior is clad in silvery-grey stained maple parquet flooring, evoking a sense of accessibility of walls and ceiling in the case of a failure of gravity. A sense of abstraction is communicated through the almost monotonous application of a surface in an unexpected location. In this sense, surface and image as carriers of information or messages are closely related.

In Zero-Gravity Space our understanding of three-dimensional space is once again being questioned. The way that the maple parquet covers the driveway, literally like a sheet of paper folded inside a box, is a clearly communicated statement: this is surface. On the other hand, a link between the notionally physical and virtual is provided: the individual parquet boards are all different in their pattern and thus refer strongly to their original nature as a material. Building the relationship between conceptual / virtual and physical materiality, the two facades towards Mutter-Ey-Strasse and the courtyard consist of large glass panels framed with stainless steel surrounds, clearly belonging to the realm of the street and thus providing a screen displaying the internal surfaces to the passer-by. Naturally, the screen effect of the end facades works in two directions and due to the dimensions of the Zero-Gravity Space dramatic perspectives are established. Looking from the inside to the outside along the homogeneous pattern of the parquet surface, the Zero-Gravity Space becomes a device for viewing and observing the external world. It is here that Zamp Kelp counteracts the physical and virtual: aware that the opacity of any building, however solid it may be, is diminished due to the constant penetration of information via telecommunications, he completely exposes the inside of the space. It may be appropriate to compare the views in and out of the space with the image of the TV screen: as a surface that is defined in its physical dimensions, providing the space for a countless number of actions and events to take place within it.

If Aldo van Eyck was enhancing the notion of inside and outside in the realm of physical space, Zamp Kelp has acknowledged the existence of the projected space and its relevance for architectural intervention.

Thus the Schmela Gallery, as it is today, presents a theoretical discourse between two architects and theoreticians, both observing contemporary phenomena of perception in their time and translating them into a built form.

Section Showing Inserted Space

Notes

* Zamp Kelp, 'Die Haut als Botschaft', in *Formalhaut*, Verlag der Georg Büchner Buchhandlung, Darmstadt, 1988, pp52–53.
1 Aldo van Eyck, quoted in Kenneth Frampton, *A Critical History of Modern Architecture*, Thames & Hudson, London, 1980, p276.
2 Zamp Kelp, 'Die Haut als Botschaft', in *Formalhaut*, op.cit, pp51–52.
3 Aldo Van Eyck quoted in Kenneth Frampton, *A Critical History of Modern Architecture*, pp276–77
4 Ibid.
5 Ibid, p277.
6 Zamp Kelp, 'Vom Monument zum Ereignis', p147.

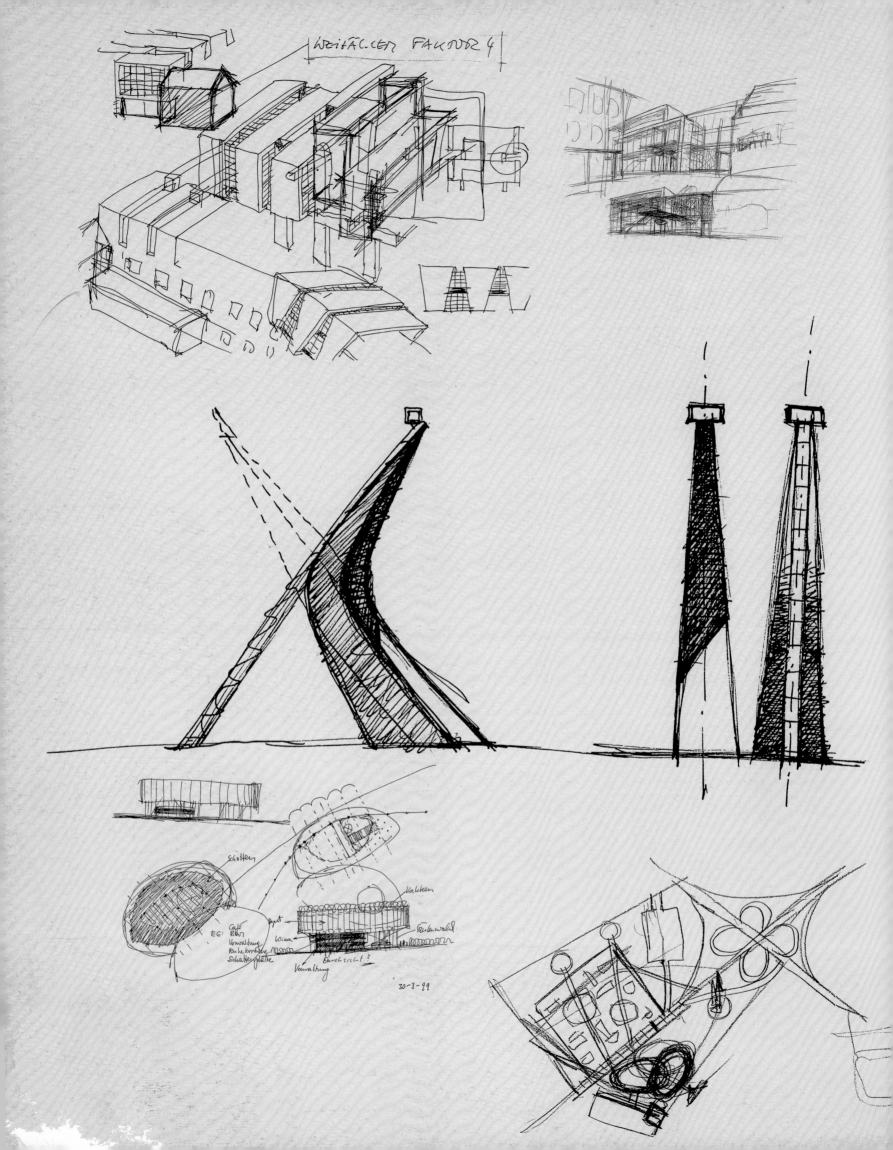

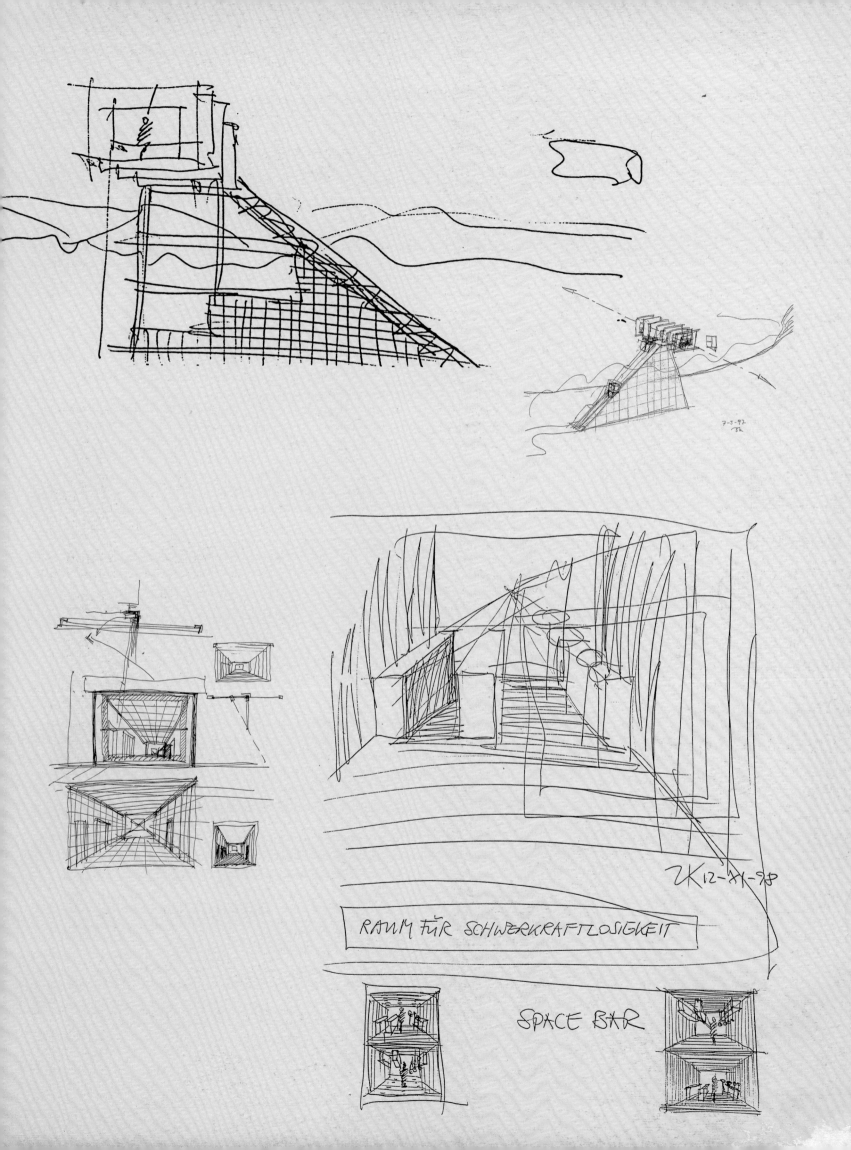

RAUM FÜR SCHWERKRAFTLOSIGKEIT

SPACE BAR

Programme, Abstraction and Figuration

Torsten Schmiedeknecht in conversation with Steven Spier

Steven Spier and Torsten Schmiedeknecht

Zamp Kelp and J.Krauss / A.Brandlhuber:
Neanderthal Museum, 1994-96,
Mettmann, Plan

Torsten Schmiedeknecht   Zamp Kelp's projects always result from a certain way of interpreting the programme. Most of his buildings provide tailor-made solutions for a specific client and a specific brief, the architect and his team assuming the role of interpreters. Despite this, he is fully aware that we live in a time of change. I believe that his projects cater for this state of flux and are strong enough to adapt. They might even have an impact on the changes. The object building can be interpreted in different ways, depending on its use. What is your way of looking at the programme and how do you interpret Zamp Kelp's strategy?

Steven Spier   Zamp Kelp's strategy towards his programme seems to be to expand it beyond an understanding as mere square meterage or offices, toilets, circulation space; to expand it to something almost metaphysical so that part of the programme becomes revealing the place or revealing the space. I think that's pretty clear in the Neanderthal Museum, where it is not restricted to the typical programme of a museum but is about something much larger. It seems to be a really useful notion about programme, and it fits in with his idea that the building is an aid to something. So although the building has a specific programme enabling it to function in the normal sense of the word, it also shows us something else, about ourselves or about the place. I think that's a sophisticated notion of function and a sensical thing. It suggests a very specific understanding of the architect's role: the architect is clearly an interpreter. Through the building, the architect has to show us something that is either profound or elemental. In the museum, for instance, Zamp Kelp shows us something of the nature of the Neander Valley and also the cultural artifact into which the Neanderthal man has been made. That's a pretty tall order and a pretty demanding brief for the architect, and it's a demanding notion of what architecture is and what a building can be. It's architecture with a capital A. You can really see how that can work in a building that is a museum, for instance. In the traditional sense of the word, it's the building as monument. But you have to wonder whether that excludes a lot of buildings from the realm of architecture because most of the city is background and most of our lives are rather mundane. So there are only moments in either the urban environment or in our own lives when architecture, in that sense, is appropriate. I'm not too clear about this, but it does raise Loos' distinction between building and architecture, and whether architecture is then restricted to a very small number of significant types of construction.

TS   Zamp Kelp made a similar point in the interview that we did last year. When I asked him about the matrix and the monument, he said in a way he would agree to that. I think that he believes in that distinction between certain programmes. As opposed to what you said, though, in his design for a House behind a River Landscape, he's not just designing a house but attempting to manifest something; he's trying to extend the programme of the house by the way that he's dealing with the facade and with the use. The brief almost looks like it falls into the commercial realm of projects.

SS   But it's clearly in a different realm to the Neanderthal Museum or Libeskind's Jewish Museum where the meaning becomes so profound and so elemental. Housing is just a much more humble sort of architecture.

Zamp Kelp: House behind a River Landscape,
Düsseldorf, 1992

When Zamp Kelp deals with
public buildings, he tries to
leave his mark, to use
metaphor and to create a
collective identity; he tries
to give something to the
public.

Housing Estate in Stockwell,
South London

TS   When Zamp Kelp deals with public buildings, he tries to leave his mark, to use metaphor and to create a collective identity; he tries to give something to the public.

SS   To create something for the public to coalesce around. But before you talked about his strategy being like Nouvel's: the intensification of the existing as opposed to simulation, which is interesting. As a strategy it's very powerful, but if the situation is really mundane, really unpleasant, or ugly, well then the strategy is slightly problematic. In the museum, the situation is so incredibly rich but what about if you're looking here, at Stockwell, in South London? What would a strategy to intensify that mean? What would that bring?

TS   I think you'd probably have to distinguish between two means of intensification. One is the visual, which you can deal with in the facade. The other is the spatial, the physical way of dealing with it, which is what Zamp Kelp does. Often he brings people up to a certain height so they can overlook the situation. In some of the museum projects, he cuts a slab out of the ground, lifts it up and then treats the edges in a certain way so you get the feeling that the building really is rooted in the site and that's partly what I meant about intensification.

SS   Well that's derived from the situation, though it's derived from the programme as well – it gets complicated. The Neanderthal Museum is really interesting because the facade and the form are rather abstract. You've got all that resort-style Hansel and Gretel type architecture around there, so the strategy of creating the opposite of what exists is a kind of intensification as well: it makes you see that gingerbread architecture for what it is by rejecting rather than assuming its style. All that is a very close and intelligent reading of the context, and a pretty profound understanding of the brief. Here Zamp Kelp really understands the programme and that generates rather remarkable results. In that building his methodology seems at its clearest and produces the best results. But there are also times when he seems to struggle with that methodology, in housing for instance, where it becomes more problematic.

TS   I think that's when he moves away from spatial treatment to abstraction – it's a very fine line. He believes in abstraction as a means to achieve these results, though sometimes he does move away from it and I think that's probably when it becomes a bit problematic. In the scheme for an International Art Museum on Lanzarote, for instance, there are two parts. One is the broken lance where he clearly moves away from abstraction and becomes almost picturesque . The other is the slab which he cuts out of the ground, lifts up 8m and clads in volcanic stone. And he makes reference to Cesar Manriquez, who basically created the island, by covering the roof in red cacti and solar panels. I think if you compare that to the lance, it's an entirely different thing. In one case it isn't even metaphorical: he's just dealing with the situation; he looks at the materials that he can find; he looks at the programme and translates it into something fairly abstract – but still recognisable. With the lance he does something quite different: it's like a massive gesture.

*Zamp Kelp: Museum Lanzarote, Competition 1999,
View of the Broken Lance*

SS   He does rely on metaphor quite a bit as a design tool. There is a difference, though, between metaphor and gesture, and in the Lanzarote scheme you can clearly see that distinction. They're not the same things: a metaphor is literally a word or phrase denoting one kind of thing in place of another to suggest an analogy between them. There is an almost alchemical process whereby the metaphor makes something into something else, it doesn't stand for something else. That's what Merleau-Ponty means when he says that the rose is love. The metaphor collapses those elements almost into one, thereby the metaphor becomes the thing. The Neanderthal Museum shows this really clearly because you can talk about it. You can talk about the metaphor of the ramp but you don't need the metaphor because the ramp is a form which takes us up to the big projection box: the form and the metaphor meld into each other and so it is not a gesture but in Lanzarote you see the two things side by side. The slab through the metaphor becomes a piece of architecture and it's almost – dare I say it – unmediated. Your experience of that building will be different according to the knowledge you bring. If you understand that nature is also culture, if you understand the history of the island and that the flora is just as artificial as the buildings then Zamp Kelp's proposal will speak to you at that level; even if you don't know that, it will be just as powerful because it will offer you something else. The same thing with the museum. The building can operate at lots of levels and that's the richness of the metaphor; you can't pick it apart when it's like that because it's melded into one, whereas the gesture is something you can take or leave – you don't get that much sustenance from it. It's a bit like having a sweet; it's rather good but you just want another one in twenty minutes or so.

Architecture can work on an emotional, physical, spatial, intellectual or conceptual level; it can hit all those things and that's the potential strength of working with metaphor. Even though Zamp Kelp sees the architect as an artist and architecture as a rarefied object, it can still speak on a lot of different levels. It doesn't have to be exclusive. It's not necessarily an architect's architecture. However, you can overdo metaphor. I am by nature slightly suspicious of the use of metaphor because it can become really self-indulgent and the danger is that you get more interested in the metaphor than in the architecture. When the metaphor and the architecture become the same thing, then it's really powerful, but it can stop at the level of a kind of intended metaphor – or even worse, the building becomes a kind of illustration of a narrative, and then you almost need a script to go through it.

TS   The narrative is quite a good point. The interesting thing about that, from my understanding, is that post-modernism is about the negation of the meta-narrative. Post-modernism or post modernity is about plurality and not having that one narrative towards which everything is going – as opposed to modernism. That's what I find interesting about Zamp Kelp's work, that he's a modernist in a way. Maybe because he's using the narrative, I see him as a modernist. On the other hand, I see the way that he deals with his architecture stylistically as postmodern.

SS   Well it's modernist in that it's a heroic definition of the architect. His buildings are incredibly ambitious. In this age, we seem so tentative: we've all been so beaten down into thinking that we can't offer much, that we can't really change things. Zamp Kelp still has an attitude which is incredibly refreshing: you can go in there and do it – and that's a modernist attitude. The post-modernist part is that each project is approached on its own merits and I guess that comes if part of the architecture is about establishing a sense of identity. Then each project has to be started from its own merits, but then each one is also bound to have a different outcome. So instead of having style as the consistent element, Zamp Kelp keeps as his constants ambition and an approach based on establishing identity or place.

TS   I think it comes from observation and that's what's carried through from his earlier work with Haus-Rucker-Co. Even when they were into the bubbles, not all of them were really designed for specific places. Quite often they would observe

Zamp Kelp's work is clearly optimistic because if he's going to reveal something to us about ourselves, what is being revealed is presumably a very positive thing. When he talks about the space of projection, clearly the presumption is that we are lesser somehow because we are so bombarded with imagery that we have lost the space in which to project ourselves. Clearly, if we do get to project ourselves that's a positive and worthwhile endeavour, so there's a basic optimism in the individual's worth. It's not at all cynical.

a place and say OK, this is what we're going to do here. Because it was only temporary, the question of style was never really an issue. It had to be radical.

SS   The earlier work also seemed more concerned with the individual. The Mind Expanding Programme, for instance, accepted the built environment. It was what it was, so you would try to change perception or to heighten the awareness of the individual. It's all designed at the scale of the individual. The interest in heightening one's awareness of where you are, and also of how you move through the world and your perception of it is still in Zamp Kelp's work, but now he expresses it more through the object and less through the individual. The object will of course also change the individual but there's a big difference between designing a bubble which is not going to be there or the cake which is going to be eaten and a big building which is mediated by all sorts of events.

TS   One of the major distinctions is that Haus-Rucker-Co's projects were always for two individuals, all their machines like the Mind Expander were for two people.

SS   It was all about a social space.

TS   Yes, in the Ballon Für Zwei a couple got engaged. It was like seeing the world through the installations: it would literally alter your perception. The nature of a building is different to the nature of a bubble. The building is there and so are you. But with the Neanderthal Museum, what that skin does when you look at it from the outside is very similar to what the skin of the bubble did when you were inside looking out: it alters your perception of your environment. It is so abstract that it's very difficult to tell how high it is if you don't know how long the panels are.

SS   Maybe what you're suggesting is that it's just the scale that has changed: that it's no longer two people in a bubble but 200,000 people visiting this museum every year. That's a huge difference in scale which changes all sorts of things.

TS   One thing that has remained consistent is his very positive approach. Even though the early work was provocative, it was very optimistic, and this is something Zamp Kelp maintains.

SS   Clearly. Archigram, too: that stuff is just happy – the idea that the Walking City is going to bring fun to places which are dreary and everyone in those drawings is always smiling. Zamp Kelp's work is clearly optimistic because if he's going to reveal something to us about ourselves, what is being revealed is presumably a very positive thing. When he talks about the space of projection, clearly the presumption is that we are lesser somehow because we are so bombarded with imagery that we have lost the space in which to project ourselves. Clearly, if we do get to project ourselves that's a positive and worthwhile endeavour, so there's a basic optimism in the individual's worth. It's not at all cynical. I was thinking about this when we were talking before about the intensification of what's there. There's a real interest again in the everyday. People like Tony Fretton and Caruso St John have rediscovered the Smithsons. Although the Smithsons' view was a bit different; it wasn't so optimistic, because what they saw when they looked at the everyday was a rather dismal thing. The problem with Brutalism is that there's a funny kind of move there. They said, well the world is a pretty grey, poor and awful kind of place (in London at least)and we're going to make our buildings rather uninviting. You start with a basic notion of humanity and you just bounce it back.

TS   When discussing the Smithsons, I think what nobody in this country ever says is that the ability of the designer is crucial and I'm not quite sure how gifted the Smithsons really were.

Archigram: Tuned Suburb, Ron Herron, 1968

A & P Smithson: Robin Hood Gardens, London, 1966-72

SS   I agree. Recently, I went to Robin Hood Gardens. It is rough, a lot of very questionable moves not only conceptually but architecturally. Around the corner Erno Goldfinger built an estate, and it is a beautiful building. I don't know quite what the architecture has to do with it, but Goldfinger's is a much more salubrious environment. Robin Hood Gardens is a dodgy place where you are scared out of your wits.

TS   A similar attitude but a very different outcome. I think some people should remain thinkers and not become designers. I think Zamp Kelp is a very skilful designer: he can master things and craft his objects well. Jean Nouvel was probably one of the first architects after the seventies to rediscover that and use industrial materials in a way where you could actually see the link to the everyday and it would give you a thrill. There is a bit of a contradiction in Zamp Kelp's work. With Haus-Rucker-Co there was the idea of bridging the gap between art and life. Now he's dealing with object buildings. You can look at it from either side. You could say he achieves both with the Neanderthal Museum; on the other hand, you could say it's very clearly in the realm of high architecture, as you say, architecture with a capital A.

SS   That seems to be his understanding of architecture but I hope he would argue that he is the professional: he's the person who's trained in this art. Furthermore, if he's not a genius, then he is at least able to see things that other people aren't. In Britain, the notion of the architect as the professional is really under attack, the notion of the architect as someone who is specifically trained, able to read and then respond to cultural issues. Zamp Kelp can assume both of those things. That the architect is allowed to be the professional and allowed to do what the architect is trained to do.
    I want to come back to the notion of the everyday. It is really complicated. What is the everyday? For Venturi, it is the brash, loud commercial architecture of the sign while for the Smithsons it was something else. For Zamp Kelp, it seems, the everyday means a kind of genuine experience, an unmediated experience. In his terms, that is something that has maybe even been squeezed out of the everyday but which actually does belong, or should belong, to our everyday existence.

TS   He clearly acknowledges the existence of mediation and of the mediated experience. We can't deny that that experience exists and we can't get rid of it – that's the notion of projected space – so how can we use the projections to establish these new identities? With identity there's always the problem of authenticity.

SS   As soon as you hear about authentic experience you're rushing down this phenomenological pathway and pretty soon bump up against Heidegger. Maybe the way Zamp Kelp gets around that is that he has never been afraid of technology. The facade in the Neanderthal Museum is a sophisticated curtain; he's not trying to build the Primitive Hut. Maybe that's the way round the regressive nature of that whole idea: you don't blink when you hear the word technology. You can use the tools that are all around us. Zamp Kelp talks about the performance of Mozart's unfinished Requiem in Vienna watched by a family: the son watches it in Stephansplatz on a big screen; the father at home on TV and the mother in the cathedral. They're all having a very different experience; each of those experiences is authentic. In one sense, a Mozart symphony is not an authentic experience even if you play it on period instruments in a period room wearing period clothes. In another sense, all those experiences are authentic and the one that is the lowest tech, in the cathedral, is not necessarily the best one.

TS   Zamp Kelp argues that the son in the square has the best experience ...

SS   Because he gets a complexity of experience: all those contradictions and complexities of playing the Requiem in that time, in that place that he's confronted with. Whereas everyone else is able to ditch some of those complexities and have a much less rich experience in the end.

Torsten Schmiedeknecht: Projection Reflection, Darmstadt, 1996

TS   One of the Haus-Rucker-Co manifestoes says that we're living in bodies of the nineteenth century but we're confronted with phenomena and technologies of the twenty-first century, so the aim is to help us to adapt to the circumstances. There's a lot of that. Many of our physical or even mental capacities have still not caught up with what is there. Thus Zamp Kelp asks how we can combine the projected elements, or the elements of the projected space, and the physical space, to give us the kind of experience that affords a better understanding of the situation.

SS   That leads us to his insistence on abstraction. He flirts with figuration but he does say in other places that he wants to use abstraction to facilitate awareness. With projected space, he says that you've got to cool down the urban environment; you have to create something which is rather more generic and stripped down to give the individual enough room to enter it. That's a really interesting idea. Every time I'm in a Frank Lloyd Wright building, I know exactly what Zamp Kelp is talking about because I'm so oppressed by the architecture. Frank Lloyd Wright is such a bully. There is no room for me in his architecture. You're just supposed to marvel at it, which I presume is what people like about it. That's an extreme case. Zamp Kelp is talking about the culture of the image.

TS   Well the abstraction. In his essay on 'Public (Societal) Space (Realm) and the Additional Element' he refers to Malevich, to the black square. It's one of his key texts. In it he compares the black square to the television screen as opposite ways of projecting things. You project your thoughts on to the black square whereas the television screen ...

SS   ... is spitting them out at you.

He sees the facade of the Neanderthal Museum as a surface for projection, but then in one of the pavilions for the Millennium View it was intended that there would be a glass floor, beneath which would be projections of capital cities – live projections, aerial views – which I thought was an interesting idea.

TS   He sees the facade of the Neanderthal Museum as a surface for projection, but then in one of the pavilions for the Millennium View it was intended that there would be a glass floor, beneath which would be projections of capital cities – live projections, aerial views – which I thought was an interesting idea.

SS   I think he's not entirely sure about this whole issue of abstraction versus figuration which, ironically, is the strength of his work because it's a really complicated issue and he's trying to resolve it. His architecture is trying to reach people; it's trying to operate at a number of levels. Figuration in architecture is very problematic. He is keen on abstraction partly because some of the things he's trying to reintroduce to people are, by definition, abstract notions. Figuration assumes a common language. Neo-Classicism works; it used to work because it expressed a common set of dominant values. Venturi can accept figuration and symbolism because he draws on the commercial vernacular. For Venturi, that is also the dominant culture and he's very comfortable with that and he thinks that architects are just too uptight to accept it. It's fun; it reflects American popular culture and, of course, it's cheap. The architect can just do it on the surface. Who wants to spend a lot of money on architecture anyway? Venturi gets around that problem. Zamp Kelp would probably say that the values he brings to building are abstract (so you can't get them in figuration)and that they are kind of in resistance to the ubiquity of the image and commercialism. So then to draw on those things if they are the only legitimate iconographic language would obviously be problematic.

TS   The term popular culture implies that it is something that is within the populace and that is what culture is. If we leave that unchallenged, it starts with the idea of the peasant who just builds his house according to his needs (if he was in the Swiss Alps, he would have a pitched roof because of the snow, for instance). It is what people are surrounded by and that is their experience. Now we're surrounded by either the high street or the big out-of-town shopping centre, overlaid with all these projected experiences and the private has become public through television and the media. Would you say that the high street is like the peasant vernacular in a way because it's the environment that we live in? What has changed is that we've lost control over it, the individual or the populace has lost control because of the profession of the architect?

SS   It's a twentieth-century problem. We've got the notion of the popular. The notion of the populace is a fairly recent invention, maybe that's the crux of the whole issue. You have a huge middle class, a huge populace which is not particularly interested in architecture, and which is building without the architect. By sheer numbers that dominates the built environment; it becomes the thing which defines us and which we all share. It's not designed by the profession, however, but is in the most cynical way what the punters want. Venturi recognises that, but he still wants to be the architect. What he's trying to do is understand what's really out there and to make sense of the contemporary condition. In an article entitled 'Chaotic Integration and its Valid Aesthetic',[1] Venturi talks about Tokyo – about how much he loves Tokyo because it can accept all of these complexities and contradictions. He talks about how it doesn't try to make sense of them, but embraces the ambiguities of scale, space, form and symbolism. It's not afraid of iconography

The way that we're experiencing the world is very much through surfaces. Some people deal with it in a purely visual way, others deal with it in a more tactile way and it's still surface but it's more complex.

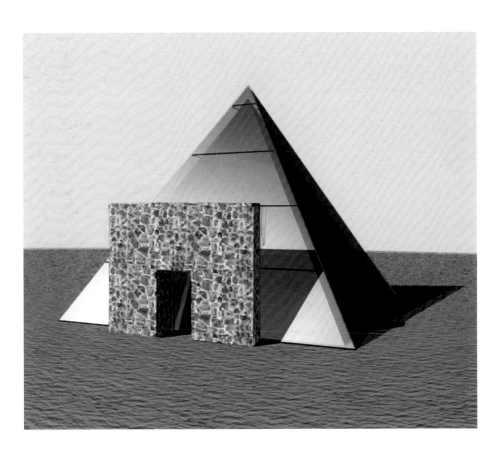

Zamp Kelp: Pavilion Millennium View

and it's not in bondage to abstraction. He sees Tokyo as unique in this respect, but thinks that it's a model for what the city could be: the ultimate kind of collage.

TS   The way that we're experiencing the world is very much through surfaces. Some people deal with it in a purely visual way, others deal with it in a more tactile way and it's still surface but it's more complex.

SS   I guess we're back to this distinction between figuration and abstraction. Both are interested in the flatness, in the surface of the image. It's partly cultural. My guess would also be that it has something to do with fashion in architecture. Modernism was still being taught in architecture schools through the sixties, if not through the seventies, and with Modernism, you're teaching space really. This interest in the surface is a kind of reaction because surface got left behind in all that stuff.

TS   Quality as well?

SS   Surface full stop. I think the character of the modernist architectural education was that you would just draw plans until you were blue in the face and then the section. It was all about the space. No-one used the term facade until the eighties with the revival of historicism. Before that you had an elevation and that's real different. It just came out of the plan; you sure didn't work on the elevation or on the facade. I think it's partly that we are a very image-driven culture right now, so we're interested in surface, but it's also a backlash against all the things that education left behind. And, of course, building technology has become very sophisticated in terms of materials for the facade.

TS   So it's both about surface as a two-dimensional image and also it's still about depth. When you look at modernism, the facade is detached and clearly separated from the structure. This is not necessarily the case anymore. What people are interested in now is the depth of the actual facade.

SS   It's interesting what technology has done. For a long time, the elevation became thinner and thinner but now, especially because of environmental considerations, there are incredibly deep facades.

TS   Exactly. Speed also becomes quite crucial if you look at a city facade. Venturi, the size and scale of things. If an office building has a deep facade, when you drive past it, it gives you the possibility to perceive more.

SS   It is interesting, though, that we are increasingly obsessed with the facade. There are building types where the only place the architecture is, is the facade. On any spec office building, even if it's high quality, all the architect gets to design are the facade and the lobby. That's it. Everything else is designed by somebody else. That's another reason why architecture has moved into the surface, because that's where the opportunity for the architecture is in a lot of ways.

TS   Yet in British schools of architecture, there is a real weakness in the treatment and teaching of facades and elevations. Quite a lot of people – especially in some London schools – still argue that the facade is the least important drawing.

SS   As you move through the city, the facade is the thing that you're experiencing. With my students, we read about Otto Wagner's interest in the modern space of the street and how he was opposed to Camillo Sitte, who wanted to construct a kind of a public space as the space of the polis. Wagner said, 'What are you talking about? In the modern street, everyone is in motion; everyone is moving and that's the public space. We don't sit around in squares debating great issues. We are too busy for that.' So the wider the avenue, the grosser the detail had to be because of the sheer scale of things, and as the building went up, you could ditch

Tokyo

Yet in British schools of architecture, there is a real weakness in the treatment and teaching of facades and elevations. Quite a lot of people – especially in some London schools – still argue that the facade is the least important drawing.

Oxford Street, London

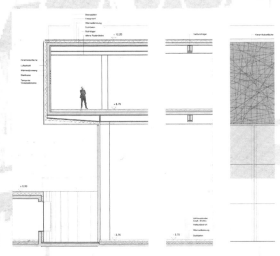

Zamp Kelp: Archaeological Museum, Herne, Competition, 1997

the detail because you couldn't see it any more. This idea that in the modern city we are moving all the time is what Venturi deals with in *Learning from Las Vegas*.

TS   I think that Zamp Kelp deals with it. When the duck comes in again at Lanzarote.

SS   Yes, it is Venturi's duck in a way: it's architecture as sculpture. But Zamp Kelp talks about the facade being the thing that we experience.

TS   As the medium.

SS   That is the thing that we experience. It comes back to the question of what to do with the facade when it can be separated from the structure, when it becomes an independent element. What does the facade do? What is its purpose? What does it communicate? These are questions that have been around since Corbusier's five points and we've been chewing them over ever since. Zamp Kelp comes up with both answers. You can cool it down and make it rather abstract, because it is like Malevich's black square. It allows you to project on to it because it becomes a sort of vast nothingness which can then be written on. Whereas Venturi says it actually needs to speak to us and, asking which language we all speak, finds it to be the commercial vernacular. Zamp Kelp sort of combines the two.

TS   But Venturi doesn't say that the facade has to communicate what is behind it, does he? It is very clearly related to the public realm. I think that is quite important. Zamp Kelp's competition entry for Herne Archaeological Museum was clad in broken ceramic tiles, like crazy paving with ceramic tiles. When you look at the drawing, you don't know what it is. The same is true of the International Art Museum on Lanzarote, where he uses the volcanic stone as the cladding material, in quite a rough way. What's intriguing there is what he doesn't do: even though he says the facade has become an independent medium in the urban landscape, he doesn't detach it – unlike Corbusier.

SS   There is still the problem of figuration and abstraction. There's the technology that allows you to have images on a glass facade, like his installation Water, Light, Vegetation at the Veterinary University in Vienna. There he's trying to figure out what to do with the facade. Although it's a figurative image, it's handled in a way in which it becomes abstract.

TS   What is interesting about that facade is that it's very thin. It's really just these panels, and they're transparent. You get a lot of views through the facade so, while it is the carrier of the image, it also establishes the relationship between the inside and the outside. So it is very tectonic; it's clearly an architectural tool. What is clever is his use of the screen both as a physical barrier and as a purely visual element – almost like an installation which really challenges your perception of what you're seeing. He is experimenting with the idea of the facade.

SS   Zamp Kelp's work recognises the difficulty in choosing between abstraction and figuration. I think that is a very fair description of where we are. His idea that abstraction is the obvious tool to counter our overwhelmingly visual and figurative environment is a really winsome argument. However, as Venturi has said, the problem with abstraction, purity and Minimalism and all those modernist devices is that they're all based on an idea of universalism. So abstraction is somehow in contradiction to Zamp Kelp's other interests: the specificity and identity of place, and the individual experience. That's the contradiction we all live with. It's not really a criticism of his work. I think it's an accurate description of where our culture is. We carry those contradictions with us all the time. Now with LED technology, you can literally make the facade a billboard. Then figuration becomes much less attractive because where is the space where you're not bombarded with the image? There's recently been a proposal – talk about a bad idea – to create a series of lit images on the walls of the tube tunnels in London. You could be in a tube and see a movie, but instead of the frames moving, you're moving. It's fantastically clever but, first of all, what are you going to see? It's obviously going to be a commercial. The second thing is, where will there be a space where you're not bombarded by that? Do I have to be assaulted by the image at every moment? Is there no space at all where I can get away from it?

It's an image-based identity in the end. He understands how an image works and he understands how you have to sell something to give it an identity.

TS   No because, even when you're at home, you have a newspaper, the TV, or the radio – and that's the most creative medium. Mind you, in Paris, the warehouse C & A has got ads in the tunnel: big signs – red, blue and yellow or something – and they're really brightly painted. You go past and you just see them for a split second.

Zamp Kelp's competition entry for the Fiege Headquarters at Osnabruck Airport uses the company's logo as the basis for the structural make-up of the building. The building itself is like a hexagonal logo. Set on its artificial hill, it also looks like a shuttle bus coming along. He achieves the figurative and abstract at the same time; it's really quite extraordinary. That's all that advertising is about. You make choices and you choose what appeals, and one of the things Zamp Kelp is interested in is corporate identity. Just as he concentrated on identity at the Neanderthal Museum, so he pursues the same idea when it comes to commercial interests. His thesis is that whatever fails to establish an identity in the next twenty or thirty years will just disappear, whether it's a city, or a firm, or a place. That moves away from the notion of authenticity to image.

SS   But that only shows that authenticity is a complicated notion. In the Neanderthal Museum, Zamp Kelp accepts that the valley has been transformed physically. The natural landscape is only natural in that it is nature, but now it's been transformed. There's probably not a square metre in Europe that has not been walked on, that has not been transformed by humans, so he recognises that it is constructed as well. It is elemental.

TS   It's an image-based identity in the end. He understands how an image works and he understands how you have to sell something to give it an identity. He's learned the lessons of advertising, and he applies them to his architecture. Though, of course, depending on need, use and client, his architecture should be longer lasting than an advertising campaign.

SS   But it's not completely cynical.

TS   No.

London, Southbank University, 22 May 1999.

Steven Spier studied philosophy at Haverford College, Philadelphia, and worked in book publishing and television production before attaining a masters degree in architecture from the Southern California Institute of Architecture. He has practised in Los Angeles, Berlin and still occasionally in London. He has taught at the ETH-Zurich at SCI-Arc in Ticino and at South Bank University, London.

He has recently been appointed Professor at the school of Architecture, Strathclyde University, Glasgow. He writes on issues in contemporary Swiss architecture, urbanism, and on the work of William Forsythe and the Ballett Frankfurt.

Torsten Schmiedeknecht: Cityscapes, Darmstadt, 1995

Note

1 Robert Venturi and Denise Scott Brown, 'Chaotic Integration and its Valid Aesthetic' in Stephen Speer (ed), *Urban Visions: Experiencing and Envisioning and the City*, Liverpool University Press and the Tate Gallery, Liverpool, 1999.

Expanding Space

Zamp Kelp

Distances and volumes, in the sense of a classical understanding of space, are disappearing. This is not the case for the individual perception. On the contrary, we are confronted with an increasing choice of spatial experiences that have to be processed. The disappearance of distances regarding the time / space relationship leads to an expansion of the individual's realm of perception.

Haus-Rucker-Co: Route to Lillyput, 1976

On a trip with my students to Shanghai, I discovered a historical roll painting in the city museum. The painting was by Peng Shunging, executed during the Ming Dynasty. It shows a man sitting at a mountain stream, reading a book. The painting's title had been translated as *Reading on a Mountainstream*. The running water stands for the stream of words flowing past the man's eyes.

A similar representation referring to our contemporary everyday would show a river that has burst its banks, from which parts of the landscape stick out like islands. A man would be sitting on one of these islands, with a closed book lying next to him. The man would be looking out for information in the medial river that has become an ocean. He would probably be looking out for a means by which he could orientate himself in the new spatial circumstances.

Painting and its derivatives illustrate the changed relationship between the representational / physical and virtual elements in our perception. In the last thirty years, there has been a quantitative shift from physical to virtual and projected perceptions. In these respects, the sixties – in their pursuit of new forms of perception and experience – were visionary. The urge to discover new realms and worlds of perception was very strong and there were many experiments to find ways in which people could gain these new experiences. Aldous Huxley's *The Doors of Perception* for instance, was one of the books that was closely studied at the time.[*] Scientific theories to expand the human field of perception by using drugs were tested in practice.

The Mind Expanding Programme of Haus-Rucker-Co, applying analogous concepts, was pursued without the help of drugs. From 1967 onwards, a series of prototypes was developed, aimed at the irritation of human perception and thus opening up extended possibilities for new experiences.

Filters of perception, situated between the human organs of perception and the everyday environment, were used to alter the user's perception. In a seemingly safe and ordered world, the conceptual aim was to conquer new phenomena of space and perception. In the sixties and seventies, the objective was to project the future. Thirty years later, these projections have become reality with immense power. The expansion of our realm of perception through projected media represents a potential with which we will have to learn to deal. The term 'space' will have to be redefined. Space is not only located outside the human body: it also emerges, due to projected image worlds, within the human brain, where these external projections are processed into worlds of experience that, in their current form, have not existed for long. Distances and volumes, in the sense of a classical understanding of space, are disappearing. This is not the case for the individual perception. On the contrary, we are confronted with an increasing choice of spatial experiences that have to be processed. The disappearance of distances regarding the time / space relationship leads to an expansion of the individual's realm of perception.

Thus, although objectively space is vanishing, subjectively it is expanding. Space projections, generated by television and computer, emerge from the movement between physical reality and representation.[1] Computers and monitors are the mediators between physical reality, projection and the perceiving individual. They create models of new or existing realities. Objectively, it seems certain that this chain of relationships is leading to the reduction of spatial distances. At the same time, it is causing an expansion of the subjective realm of perception, leaving the individual stressed and disorientated.

What are the answers that the physical and representational part of the world can give to these problems in which the artificial is being increased by the virtual? From the very beginning, artificiality has been a characteristic part of architecture. Architecture is an invention of man which, while fulfilling practical needs like shelter, has always been a medium of communication for man's myths, religions and power structures. Having always had an element of representation, architecture historically fulfilled similar needs to those that the computer does today. Modernism and the later increase of media factors have changed architecture's role regarding representation. The contents of a possible second modernism have been much discussed in the eighties and nineties. One of its tasks will be to structure this newly emerged variety into understandable elements or parts.[2] The creation of aura through the means of media will play a major part in rebuilding socially problematic areas. Another factor is the creation of a physical-virtual realm of experience, contributing to a constructive development of social awareness. Neither of these elements should be seen exclusively, but they are models for a practice that, if applied specifically, can have an impact on the relationship between the physical and virtual – the projective parts of society.

Awareness (Consciousness) and the Cultural Landscape [3]

According to Buckminster Fuller, the minimal description of life is 'awareness'. Awareness consists of at least one system that becomes aware and another system that is being perceived by the first one. Therefore, awareness is the sum of four elements: the observer, the observed, the line of thought that connects the two, and the void around which the thing is being observed. Considering this scientifically, the void is Fuller's geometrical space within which the biological space emerges through the installation of activity. Thus the environment in which we live can be classified as biological and geometrical space, the two referring to each other with variable intensity. Biological space exists as a chain of events that causes movement putting the surrounding geometrical space – for instance architecture – on stage, merging both into illuminated, changing, spatial unity.

Architecture protected man from different external threats. The transport of information into the most remote locations now penetrates the idea of 'shelter' in our consciousness. At the end of the twentieth century, the speed of perception is being altered by a new phenomenon. Not a single moment in our daily lives is free from the informative projection of real or fictive stories. Whether a Walkman creates another layer on our way through the city or a TV-screen projects public life into the privacy of living rooms, the space of projection occurs as the third element next to biological and geometrical space. Thus our understanding of the cultural landscape is being altered.

Architecture remains static in the physical sense. However, the addition of projections and projected space on to our daily reality makes us experience the same stable architectural elements in a different way every day. After the invention of the railway, we had to alter our systems of perception and another change is now necessary. However, as opposed to the railway experience, when the landscape started racing past the carriage, we do not need to move to experience the new dimensions of perception. Whether we want it or not, the world of information is

Haus-Rucker-Co: Yellow Heart, Vienna, 1968

Zamp Kelp: Green Glass Surface,
Düsseldorf, 1995-96

Zamp Kelp: Mekka Medial,
Paris 1990, Model

passing in front of us and, like a camera, our awareness is choosing what to acknowledge from what is presented.

At the end of the twentieth century, we are becoming nomads again, but nomads in an inverted sense. Without having to relocate ourselves, we experience the projected world that is drifting by. Our inevitably altered sense of perception will have an impact on architecture. The often discussed farewell to the mechanised world also means a goodbye to clear and definitive contexts. Thus the role of architecture as geometrical space is about to change. Architecture has over the years given away elements of its traditional tasks. Architecture will no longer have the role of demonstrating power. The media elements of the projected space will take over this role.

Therefore, architecture's claim for the absolute has become obsolete. At the same time, new functions become visible on the horizon of perception. To visualise geographically the multitude of sociological events regarding their time-space relationship will be one of architecture's new tasks. Cityscape becomes legible at its surfaces. This is where architecture has the chance to react to changes in biological and geometrical space. The architectural skin or surface has been detached from the architectural construction. The surface has become an independent and flexible medium in the urban landscape. Via the architectural surface the attempt is being made to establish a new relationship between the new and the old parts of public space.

Public (Societal) Space (Realm) and the Additional Element [4]

In 1925, Malevich published his introduction to the theory of the additional element in painting. He describes how a new structural element enters an existing artistic system and thus starts to alter and mould it. This theory is also relevant in observing current tendencies in the development of society. Just as in painting, Cubism abolished the object in its quest for purity, so society and its components are losing their relationship with the representational (physical) because of the newly arrived phenomenon of medial projection. Malevich's *Black Square* (1914) is today opposed by the opaque rectangle of the television screen, both providing surfaces for infinite numbers of projections. However, the projections in both cases are directed in opposite directions. The black square, being the screen for the projection of signs and images resulting from thought processes inside the infinite space of the human brain, serves as an intermediate location for thoughts on the way to the possible realisation of ideas. By contrast, the television screen is the medium of a gigantic medial network whose task it is to inform about anything, at any time, and in any place.

The abstract concepts of modern art in regard to abolishing the object are becoming reality in the current public realm through the means of projection. However, unlike in modernism where the object was also eliminated thematically, objects and the representational through the omnipresent projection of their images play an important role in the realm of media. We have already seen that the public realm / sociological space used to consist of two major elements: the biological space as a chain of events and the geometrical space. Resulting from this relationship was the scenery of daily life and the tangibility of places and events. This constellation has come increasingly under the influence of the medial element: projections overlay, complete and substitute the perceivable reality of social space as we used to know it.

The black square has its three-dimensional equivalent in the Kaaba in Mecca, a black cube which is a place of communication for a whole community beyond its religious purpose. Disconnected from Islam, the cube with its infinite black volume becomes a space in which any possible representational/physical hopes and wishes of a society can be imagined, a container in which, metaphorically, all the world's fetishes are gathered. By contrast, the television screen finds itself metaphorically compared to a cubic space in which an infinite number of events can take place. An inherent characteristic of such a space is an opening on at least one side,

At the end of the twentieth century, we are becoming nomads again, but nomads in an inverted sense. Without having to relocate ourselves, we experience the projected world that is drifting by. Our inevitably altered sense of perception will have an impact on architecture. The often discussed farewell to the mechanised world also means a goodbye to clear and definitive contexts. Thus the role of architecture as geometrical space is about to change. Architecture has over the years given away elements of its traditional tasks. Architecture will no longer have the role of demonstrating power. The media elements of the projected space will take over this role.

giving the viewer access to activities taking place in its biological space. Accessibility establishes a relationship with the levels and networks of media projection that make events into an omnipresent experience for society. Projection as the new element determining space adds a new level to the relationship between place and society. Thus we are now dealing with both a physical-corporeal perception of location and an intangible one at media-level, which we can experience anywhere through media networks.

Looking at the opposition of the representational realm and the incorporeal realm of projection, it seems as if the the world is divided into two parts, with the projections aiming to destroy the objects. In doing so, there seems to be no understanding of the fact that the destruction of the object goes hand-in-hand with the end of reporting and informing about our global society, and hence projections lose their meaning. Thus the need emerges for links between tangible and projective culturally determined processes. The field of experiment for new dimensions of perception has been extended. Space and location are anachronistic without the medial network. On the other hand, without space and location, there would occur a loss of content within the transport of information from events and activities in a media-age society. Space and location in the future will have to be closely linked to medial networks.

As part of the corporeal realm, architecture will increasingly have to structure the multitude of societal corporealities within which we move. Stadia, for instance, are an example of gathering places that meet the need for changeability by host-

Haus-Rucker-Co: Centre for Arts and Media Technology, Karlsruhe, Competition, 1989

ing ever new events. The element of media within these architectures is thus being generated by the events that take place within them. Other architectural structures that until now had been built for specific purposes will not be able to keep up with the demand for rapid change. Architecture must quickly adapt itself. It must also recognise that rapid changes of content imply the need for adaptability in appearance.

Architecture thus consists of functional content and related media components which, by applying signs and symbols, imply the particular content and enable us to read and understand the spatial structure of the urban landscape.

The Phenomenon of Translocation

Presence is inherently linked with the scale of time, whereas place, in its original sense, is related to geographical circumstances. The ratio of presence to place thus depends on the relationship between time and geography which is a sum of natural laws in which the phenomena of translocation are contained. Translocation, as a part of our perception that because of present sociological developments is gaining more and more importance, can best be explained in the three following examples:

Haus-Rucker-Co: Temporary Mistakeness in Basel, 1997

1) In Egyptian high cultures, leading statesmen were regarded as being present at ceremonies or events which they could not attend, if they were substituted for by a three-dimensional life-size replica figure of themselves. Thus the 'I' of a certain personality could be identified by the attending parties in a location that was different to their place of being.

2) With the invention of the Panorama [a 360-degree painting] by Robert Barker in 1787, the geographical fixation of the notion of place came into being. The panorama as the mass media of the nineteenth century created the partial translocation of cities, landscapes and scenes of both present and past. Scenes from geographically or historically distant locations could be perceived in one place. City panoramas of London were presented in Paris and vice versa. Historical events such as the battle on the Isel Mountain in Austria gained an artistic position as a scenario beyond the notion of memory.

3) The third example describes how the notion of locality can originate from commodities. During the Second World War the US Army used to establish Coca-Cola depots ten days in advance in locations to which troops would be moved. American soldiers therefore always travelled to the known commodity, the Coca-Cola bottle, which would comfort them with a sense of identity and trust. The strategic product as a mobile part of locality and transmitter of 'translocal homeliness'.

Haus-Rucker-Co: Cover, Krefeld, 1971

All three examples contain aspects showing that locality can not only be seen in geographical terms. People, smells, atmosphere, day- and night-time, and commodities are as much part of it as the mountain tops that we want to climb. In an Italian restaurant in Germany is embedded a part of Italy and the German tourist finds part of his native home in the German food in a Majorcan holiday resort. We link certain smells with places in which we lived through a characteristic moment, perhaps in the company of someone specific, at a certain moment, under certain weather conditions. Through the 'translocal presence' of one of the ingredients that the event involved, the place of its occurrence lives on in our thoughts. The translocation of places and events from our past into the present of our awareness we call memory. The specific and physical rebuilding of places from the past we call reconstruction. The attempt to translocate places and positions from the future into the present we call simulation. Cover – Surviving in a Polluted Environment (1971), a project by Haus-Rucker-Co staged in the Museum Haus-Lange in Krefeld, was just such a simulation.

Haus-Rucker-Co attempted to visualise a position from a possible future scenario in the present of 1971 to create an awareness of possibly irreversible developments

Presence is inherently linked with the scale of time, whereas place, in its original sense, is related to geographical circumstances. The ratio of presence to place thus depends on the relationship between time and geography which is a sum of natural laws in which the phenomena of translocation are contained.

in society. A grip on the past becomes possible through materialisation of formerly existing locations. The temporary reconstruction of the Berlin Stadtschloß using painted fabric on scaffolding posts is a problematic speculation for sentimental feelings which could lead to more enduring reconstructive strategies in urban planning. Imitations of the past society produce translocation that emerges from the permanently growing spectrum of information and mobility. Countless souvenirs of buildings, monuments and symbols, like the Statue of Liberty and the Brandenburg Gates, produce translocality in the most remote places. In this context, a postcard showing the pyramids of Giza topped with the slogan 'Greetings from Düsseldorf' provides the link to the phenomena of the present culture of information which has created the potential for the omnipresent transport of locality by means of projection. Places, so it seems, are no longer a question of geographical location or position. In the age of medial projection, places are located where they can be consciously perceived. We accept the lack of materiality and play, as soon as we give in to the need for physicality and travel to new places, with the feeling of having been there before. The growing omnipresence of places creates global intimacy and monotony among locations of different cultural origins and contexts. Urban centres in Asia, like Szentschen, built on Chinese rice plantations twelve years ago, are only distinguishable from American downtowns by the different type of writing on the neon advertising boards. The global monotony of public and sociological space is opposed by society's massive need for more and more new and unexploited perceptions.

The phenomenon of translocation will grow in opposing directions. Being the cause of monotony, it will at the same time be a means to help us create the individual fields of our perception in a time-related and distinctive manner. Places that will not produce identity will vanish from our awareness. Permanent renewal and time- and space-related identity will become the premises for the vitality and prosperity of regions. The (utopian) idea of equipping places with 'identity machines', such as Mekka Medial for the Gare d'Austerlitz in Paris, become more and more realistic. The linking of such identity-building event structures with media networks, as shown in Mekka Medial, is an essential ingredient.

The symbiosis of geographical place and dynamic systems of media transport is changing the concept of public and sociological space. Locality and architecture, in its old sense, will lose meaning. Cities will artificially create their identities as flowing processes to manufacture a profile. Such urban identities can be mobile in character, like the identity created by hosting the Olympic Games. Translocality as a current phenomenon of perception therefore consists of the trinity of place, event and the transport of media. This constellation will create identities that will structure future society's awareness.

The phenomenon of translocation will grow in opposing directions. Being the cause of monotony, it will at the same time be a means to help us create the individual fields of our perception in a time-related and distinctive manner. Places that will not produce identity will vanish from our awareness.

Virtuality and Public Space

Virtuality in the form of dreams, hopes and expectations is as old as mankind. Virtuality as it confronts contemporary society is determined by endless projected information that almost demands the impossible from our senses and perception. Therefore, the desire to look back to the places of the past and to reincarnate them seems only natural. The public square as a geographical place is a means of establishing an overview in the physicality of events in the urban fabric, and may create a sense of intimacy. Simultaneously, such feelings are overshadowed by doubts as to whether the historical typology of the public square is still applicable in an age where information can instantly transform or change positions within society. It only seems to be a question of time before human perception will be able to cope with the polarity between physical city space and the constantly changing virtual space media projection. Already for most people projected experiences on television or in the cinema seem to be more real than a walk in their own neighbourhood. The televised report from a far-away place becomes more important than our current physical location. The report has a time limit, a beginning and an end, and thus alters the claim for permanence that until today has been inherent in our notion of architecture.

Zamp Kelp: Projection of Signs, Frankfurt, 1987

Zamp Kelp: Projection of Signs, Frankfurt, 1987

The relationship between space and society has changed. Similarly, the meaning of buildings, cities and landscapes in both society and our perception has shifted. The idea of home used to be related to a geographical place but has since become linked to commodities or television programmes, for example.

Architecture and society representing geometrical and biological space become parts of scenarios that through the projection of information are being perceived as limited units concerning their duration. Therefore, television or the Internet still depend on physical events in society since these events provide the content for the projected information. The event as interface between virtual and physical (real) sequences of our perception provides the premise for the synergetic coexistence of the two dominant factors in our realm of current experience. The demands on architectural and urban developments concerning the tendencies of change are thus both numerous and complex. Computer-animated images of planned architectural developments and contexts, anticipating reality in the representational sense and drawing us into a world of weightlessness, are taking the place of film architecture that until now was leading the conceptual development of future scenarios. Applying the principle of feedback, these animations determine the appearance of society's representational and physical realms. The future development of the notion of space and perception in general, and of streets and squares as public fields of expression in particular, seems to be determined by the symbiosis of representational and virtual parts. Therefore, every square, street and object, but also every human being participating in the network of communicative events, will be equipped with a medial aura creating identity. In the specific case of streets and squares, this aura will be established by cursory superposition of parts of mediated information, extending the established notion of architectural and spatial constellations. The following example of an urban square as perceived by three different observers describes how our perceptions are challenged in a multitude of ways.

On 5 December 1991, the City of Vienna was celebrating the bicentenary of the composer Wolfgang Amadeus Mozart's death. In the cathedral of St Stephan, the Viennese Philharmonic Orchestra played Mozart's unfinished Requiem. A Viennese family consumed the event in three different ways: the wife sat inside the cathedral to experience the concert in its most classical form; her husband watched the event on television in his living room at home; and their son stood outside the cathedral where the concert was shown on a big screen. The wife inside the cathedral had the least stunning audio experience. Because of the delayed sound travel in Gothic churches and the cross-shaped plan of the building, she could hear only parts of the music. Her husband, at home in his heated living room, had the best experience regarding the amount of information and quality of sound that he could hear. The most intense impression was experienced by their son standing in the square outside the cathedral where an ice-cold wind was howling and forcing people to cluster closer together, he saw the projection of the event inside the cathedral on the big screen, overlaid with the massive dark exterior of the cathedral, within the spatial arrangement of the square.

Identity, the Representational and Projection[5]

The logo of a corporation is not representative. What makes it representative is the logo's constant and repeated projection into society's realm. Through the logo's projection, awareness of the identity and potential of a corporation is generated. At the end of the twentieth century, society is influenced by omnipresent projections of media that determine our experiences. As much as the cultural landscape used to be a result of the spatial differences between city and nature, it will in the future be generated by the polarity of the representational and the virtual, projected image.

The relationship between space and society has changed. Similarly, the meaning of buildings, cities and landscapes in both society and our perception has shifted. The idea of home used to be related to a geographical place but has since become linked to commodities or television programmes, for example. The experience of a German TV-journalist who detected feelings of homesickness while watching *Dallas* on TV in a Warsaw hotel room is a clear indication of the fact that the 'idea of home' has become a more and more geographically independent phenomenon. Architecture has ceased to exist as a monumental issue that helps us orient our-

Zamp Kelp: Ornamenta 1 – Built Fiction,
Schweinfurt, 1989

selves. It has become part of time-related scenarios that consist of physical and virtual aspects. The physical monument has become irrelevant and is being replaced by the televised report about it.

If space and architecture are to maintain their position in society, they will have to adopt more event-like characteristics. Space will become the place for events and actions, with architecture and architectural surfaces providing the background for such temporary scenes, for instance, as screens for projections. Parts of the process promoting coexistence in our daily lives are fashion and advertising. The projection of advertising messages on to the surfaces of the city stimulates the consumption of physical objects and commodities by society. Fashion as a physical projection on the individual body visualises current awareness of society at a specific moment in time, and creates perspectives for the *Zeitgeist*. Therefore, fashion and advertising are destined to be catalysts which mediate in the field of physical and virtual experiences. Architecture's role in this realm is complex and multilayered. The fact that virtual spaces do not work according to the laws of gravity, construction and materiality offers a multitude of new possibilities for our perception of spatial and architectural contexts which, in combination with the physical world, may create a new spatial understanding. Within this new spatial understanding or spatial culture, our behaviour and perception gain new importance, since they have to obey the 'power of the eye'.

Built fictions in the physical space are opposed by dematerialised monuments in the virtual part of our perception. Space as experience can no longer be thought of without virtual elements, or, to put it another way, the relationship of the virtual world with the physical world becomes essential for our perception of society.

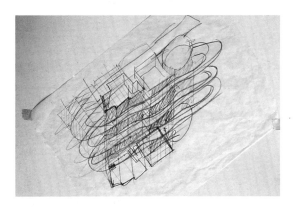

Zamp Kelp and J.Krauss / A.Brandlhuber:
Neanderthal Museum, 1994-96,
Nettmann,Conceptual Sketch

Built fictions in the physical space are opposed by dematerialised monuments in the virtual part of our perception. Space as experience can no longer be thought of without virtual elements, or, to put it another way, the relationship of the virtual world with the physical world becomes essential for our perception of society.

The Charisma of Built Formation[6]

It may be that the multitude of perceptions on offer makes our era seem as though it is without perspective and that this causes an awareness of diffuse disorientation for the inhabitants of our cultural landscape. This awareness can no longer be prevented by using only ordered and articulated architectural spaces as the realm local in society. If we allow ourselves to question the exclusiveness of geometrical space and consider mediated and projected spaces as equal factors in the structuring of local surroundings, the need for new ways of thinking regarding diversity and variety becomes evident. It seems that thinking and acting in small but significant systems of units might be an appropriate means of reaching people's awareness and of creating identity and orientation. The scenario as a tool uniting the productive parts of mediated, conceptual and representational (physical) elements of our perceptions, offers the possibility to theme and to structure the diversity to which we are being exposed. Theming is comprehensible and creates the opportunity to explain changing parameters and aims of sociological future developments. The staging inherently consists of imaginary and representative elements that visualise one-dimensional expectations and needs in three-dimensional space. In the age of computer science, elements that become relevant are those that are surrounded by the aura of the mediation (media). Specific parts of society, in the spatial sense, which do not have that aura lose their identity. In the near future, anonymous parts of our cities will have to be equipped with the above mentioned aura: they will have to become 'medial'. However, revaluation and programmatical creation of aura for existing circumstances are not always the key factors. The structuring of the new space cultures combines the complex perception on offer and establishes physical-virtual experiences that are crucial for the ongoing constructive development of awareness in society.

Such scenarios can be present in various different conditions. Depending on their nature they may occur in the network of media projection or physically in their geographical location. The latter combines the physical nature of a place with projected simulations in a specific thematic context. The architectural containers for such themed conclusions first and foremost have the task of housing the theme's collected and visualised aspects. Secondly, these buildings are to translate the present contents into built metaphors, to provide them with a tailor-made outfit. Through this combination of content and context, the localised theme becomes an experience, a simulation so to say, that considers both place and theme.

The design of the Neanderthal Museum in Mettmann, Germany, has followed these principles. Being a museum for the history of mankind, it is also a museum for the history of space and time, which have developed as vital premises for and with man. Simultaneously, the Neanderthal was the place for one of the most important archaeological finds in respect of the exploration of man's development. The museum's architecture serves as a visualisation of a theory that considers man's development as a ribbon-like movement. The museum's spiral seemingly comes out of the depths of the earth and ends tangentially, pointing in a direction of uncertainty, becoming a warning sign for future humanist perspectives. The Neanderthal Museum is at once a piece of built virtuality, architecture and event. Its semi-transparent skin signals fleetingness, whereas inside, in the compact ramped spaces, one can experience the history of man on TV monitors and through computer animations. As an entirety of architecture, content and visitors, the museum represents – in terms of the Neanderthal – the geographical place. In the wider perspective of its function regarding the content, the museum projects the history and future of the world.

City and Multi-Medial Orbit

In the previous section, we looked at the increasing impact of systems of information and media on the development of physical space within society. In the light of these phenomena, the current architectural discussion between rational tectonists and democratic constructors about the appropriate style for our time and society becomes obsolete. Neither construction nor space-related construction can, in the age of the media society, define the position of architecture and urban landscape. The appropriate means for architectural expression is situated in the realm between space, surface and construction.

Perception of surface has become part of our daily experience which is therefore linked to the communication of information. Thus urban tectonics have been replaced with the tectonics of images and identities. It has become natural to us that as elements of a second nature, architecture and urban landscape stand opposed to the dematerialised dialogue between society and media. To mediate between the representational and the immaterial projection is an elemental task that is facing the development of new ways of seeing and the strategic concepts for the complex realm of society as a whole. A new reality will emerge that will determine the character of urban landscapes within which the presence of the multi-medial orbit has become a fact. In a way that is analogous to film (where audio-visual messages are organised into frames and sequences), the city presents itself as a series of scenarios. Large 'city-frames' consist of separate parts that can be perceived independently. The individual frame remains visible in the multitude of the parts. Context emerges in the awareness of the individual due to the sequential character of the perceived environment. Thus scenes from the past can exist unproblematically alongside those from the present or the future. This is an important factor for the future determination and understanding of space and society. The creation of a permanently updated climate of perception is a key programmatic point. Climate, here, is defined as the sum of all individual frames or scenarios, be it in the representational or projected realm, that are perceivable by society. Diversity is the key to the freedom of perception and establishing opinions. Theming of the urban landscape will in this context play an important role. Whereas some cities have always operated in a conservative, past-related way, soon there will be cities that, by means of their aura, will attract progressively orientated élites and corporations.

Cities as staged frames are themed elements of our perception as much as the nine o'clock news on television. The staging takes place on the urban and architectural surfaces which include parts of the public space. It will be society's task to write a script to enable a culture of surface to take place and to act as a medi-

Facade Düsseldorf

Cities as staged frames are themed elements of our perception as much as the nine o'clock news on television. The staging takes place on the urban and architectural surfaces which include parts of the public space. It will be society's task to write a script to enable a culture of surface to take place and to act as a mediator between the multi medial orbit and the built reality, and to conduct it in such a way that the climate of change and flexibility necessary to cope with innovative and evolutionary processes will be established.

ator between the multi-medial orbit and the built reality, and to conduct it in such a way that the climate of change and flexibility necessary to cope with innovative and evolutionary processes will be established.

Urbanity and the New World Order

World society's evolution in the coming ages is unpredictable. There are tendencies that seem to suggest that with the end of the Cold War a new and more complex global network of political powers will emerge. Henry Kissinger suggests that the international system in the twenty-first century will consist of at least six super powers and supposes that these powers might be the USA, Europe, China, Japan, Russia and possibly India. According to Samuel P Huntington, society is developing towards a multi-polar and multi-cultural model in which the potential for friction and confrontation will arise from cultural differences between the power systems. Applying this theory to the development of the metropolis, it suggests that we will soon see the end of a particular kind of regionalism that is occurring not only in architecture, for instance in Germany (Berlin) and France (Paris). Groups of countries with cultural similarities will join together and develop an attitude towards architecture and urban planning as happened under the Austro-Hungarian monarchy. Society will consciously distinguish between the richness of traditional city structures and future concepts that inherently include European themes and dimensions. In Europe, architectural and urban planning will be determined by the common ground shared by the countries that culturally and politically constitute the European Union. Regarding the 'battle of cultures' between the newly emerging formations of political and cultural power, it is evident that the 'battlefields' will not be located in the physical realm, but in the realm of a multi-medial global orbit. The visualisation of orbital events requires surface: be it the translucent screens of monitors or the facades of our cities. Surfaces will become important media for the development of strategies establishing self-assertion of cultural areas. This is where the physical and representational elements of society might regain influence and once again become effective. Assuming that urban structures will account for the communication of political positions and geographical locations will serve as places for the discursive exchange of thoughts and opinions between cultures, the profile of the mediated public realm, and therefore the profile of the city, will change. The plurality of overlapping cultural dialogues will probably take place via the electronic network of information technology.[7] It is therefore possible that in the absence of direct contact, frictions will arise if the different cultural areas do not allow each other to establish individual niches while maintaining a presence in specific geographical locations. 'Diplomacy in urban planning' will be required, which means that foreign cultures will be given possibilities of presence and exchange in other cultural areas than their own.

Opposed to the communicative potential of the medial orbit will be a system of contact points in the geography of the geometrical space. The self-promotion and identity of geographical areas regarding their cultural differences will play a major role in the future, especially the ways in which these identities will be effective in the entirety of geometrical, biological and projected space. Presence, as resulting from the harmonic interplay of geometric-biological and projected elements of space in a society, becomes an existential feature in a climate of competing cultures.

Japanese Temple in Düsseldorf

Notes

* Aldous Huxley, *The Doors of Perception – Heaven and Hell*, Chatto and Windus, London, 1954–56.
1 Claude Cadoz, *Die Virtuelle Realität*, Kollektion Domino.
2 Heinrich Klotz, 'Die 2.Moderne'.German television interview on 3Sat, 2 June 1999.
3 Taken from: Zamp Kelp 'Die Haut als Botschaft', pp51–53.
4 A similar version of this text (different translation) has been published as : 'Architektur und Medialität' in *Daidalos* No 35, March 1990.
5 Taken from 'Vom Monument zum Ereignis', pp143–47.
6 Ibid.
7 Michael Erlhoff, 'Mediales Beben', *Mediale Aureolen für die Stadt*, Galerie Aedes, Berlin, 1997.

PROJECTS 1987-99

(all projects are in Germany unless otherwise stated)

1987

Fetish Room, Frankfurt. Installation at German Design Council.

Pfalztheatre, Kaiserslautern. (Haus-Rucker-Co with Thomas Gutt).

Brüser Berg, Bonn. Community Centre with Catholic and Protestant churches and kindergarten (Haus-Rucker-Co with Thomas Gutt).

Town Hall Environs, Bielefeld. Design for the extension of the town hall square (Haus-Rucker-Co).

Chrysler, Frankfurt. Design for a trade fair stand for the IAA (Haus-Rucker-Co).

Trade Fair Palace, Vienna, Austria. Competition for an urban strategy for the Messepalast area, first stage (Haus-Rucker-Co).

Hermann-Ehlers-Platz, Berlin. Proposal (Haus-Rucker-Co).

Hotel at the Victoria Premises, Berlin. Proposal for a 300-bed hotel.

Media Park, Cologne. Urban proposal for the former Gereon cargo area (Haus-Rucker-Co).

The Ideal Museum, Kassel. Project for Documenta 8 (Haus-Rucker-Co).

City Hotel Berlin. Proposal for ITAG Berlin.

Victoria Insurance, Berlin. Proposal for an administration building.

Green Cube, Vienna, Austria. Courtyard design for WIFI Wien., Vienna, Austria.

Technical Town Hall, Graz, Austria. Proposal (with D Hoppe).

Santa Monica Square, Hamm. Urban proposal.

Projection of Signs, Frankfurt. Scenario at German Design Council.

1989

Ornamenta 1. Pforzheim. Design for a jewellery exhibition.

ZKM, Karlsruhe. Competition for a centre for arts and media technology (Haus-Rucker-Co).

Electricity Substation, Cologne. Proposal.

Roof Conversion, Berlin. Project for a roof extension at the Hochschule der Künste.

Bridge Cross, Berlin. Urban proposal.

NKZ, Berlin. New centre for Kreuzberg.

Visual Machines, Nagoya, Japan. Design for a trade fair stand at the German Design Exposition (with W Laubersheimer).

Paderborn Airport. Proposal for a terminal building (with Andreas Hanke and Rodriguez Diaz).

Panorama Pavilion. Proposal for the Austrian Pavilion for the 1992 Seville Expo, 1989-90 (Zamp Kelp and Diether S Hoppe).

Mekka Medial. Project for the City and Utopia exhibition, Paris / Berlin, 1989-90.

1990

Transformation, Cologne. Proposal for a building on a bunker incorporating a work by Felix Droese.

House for the Styrian Autumn, Graz, Austria. Proposal for a symbol and accommodation for a cultural institute.

Culture Mile, Hamburg. Urban study for Deichtorplatz and Ericusspitze.

Mönnighoff Factory, Bochum. Proposal for the extension of production facilities (with Rodriguez Diaz).

Ring of Frames, Berlin. Design for a playground in Spandau.

1991

Jewellery Museum, Pforzheim. Proposal for alterations to the Reuchlinhaus (with Rodriguez Diaz).

Water, Light, Vegetation. Permanent installation at the Veterinary University Ballroom, Vienna, 1991-95.

Museum of Inland Navigation, Duisburg. Competition: commendation (with Andreas Hanke and Rodriguez Diaz).

1992

House behind River Landscape, Düsseldorf. *Proposal for a mixed-use building.*

Indoor Swimming Pool and Cycling Stadium, Berlin. Competition: mention.

Prager Street, Dresden. Competition: first prize.

Expanding Space, Meinerzhagen. Completion of an existing group of buildings (with Christoph Kessler).

1993

Dortmunder U, Dortmund. Urban proposal for restructuring a brewery (with Andreas Hanke and Rodriguez Diaz).

Neanderthal Museum, Mettmann. Competition: second prize (Zamp Kelp and J Krauss/ A Brandlhuber),1993-96.

1994

Kleist Theatre, Frankfurt/Oder. Competition entry (with J Krauss).

1995

Green Glass Surface, Düsseldorf. Entrance area for E Plus Mobilfunk Headquarters, 1995-96.

NOA, Dortmund. Proposal for a socio-ecological environment, 1995-1996.

1996

Culture Magnet, Berlin. Proposal for the Austrian Embassy in Berlin (with Professor D S Hoppe).

Rautenstrauch-Joest Museum, Cologne. Proposal.

1997

Georg Schäfer Museum, Schweinfurt. Competition entry.

Fiege Headquarters, Osnabrück. Competition entry for office and administration buildings at Airport Münster/Osnabrück.

Archaeological Museum, Herne. Competition entry.

Millennium View, Steinbergen. Cultural Park, 1997-2000.

Expo 2000 German Pavilion, Hanover. Proposal.

Primary School with Day Centre, Vienna, Austria. Proposal (with Diether S Hoppe).

1998

Donau Museum, Linz, Austria. Competition entry.

Zero-Gravity Space, Düsseldorf. Alteration of an Aldo van Eyck Building, 1998-99.

1999

International Art Museum Lanzarote, Canary Islands, Spain. Invited competition.

Niederrhein Museum, Wesel. Invited competition.

Today is Tomorrow, Bonn. Concept for a design exhibition in Bundeskunsthalle.

Exhibitions

'**Ansichten und Grundrisse**' (Elevations and Plans), Bei Lindinger und Schmid, Regensburg, 1994

'**Mediale Aureolen für die Stadt**' (Medial Aureoles for the City) Galerie Aedes, Berlin, September 1996

'**Zamp Kelp**' NAI. Netherlands Architectuurinstituut, Rotterdam, 1997

AWARDS

1979 **Kunstpreis Berlin. City of Berlin's Fine Arts Award for being a member of Haus-Rucker-Co**

1995 **Gustav Meyer Award, Berlin, for the Ring of Frames project**

1997 **Deutscher Architekturpreis Beton. German Architecture Award of the German Cemen Federation for the Neanderthal Museum**

1997 **BDA Preis. Association of German Architects' Award for good buildings**

1998 **European Museums Award**

1998 **Architekturpreis Nordrhein Westfalen. Architecture Award of the District of North Rhine-Westphalia**

PROJECT CREDITS

Ornamenta 1– Built Fiction
Design for a Jewellery Exhibition in Pforzheim, 1989.

Client: Stadt Pforzheim
Architect: Günter Zamp Kelp
Realisation: Consortium Stadt Pforzheim
Jewellery Layout: Design Students Fachhochschule Pforzheim

Water, Light, Vegetation
Permanent installation at the Veterinary University, Vienna, 1991-95.

Client: Österreichisches Bundesministerium für Wirtschaftliche Angelegenheiten
Architect: Günter Zamp Kelp
Contact Office Vienna: Architekt Heinrich Eidenböck

Millennium View
Steinzeichen - Steinbergen, Cultural Park Steinbergen, 1997-2000.

Client: Josef Wärmer, Schaumburger Steinbrüche, Steinbergen
Concept: Andreas Groß and Günter Zamp Kelp
Project Leader: Andreas Groß
Architect: Günter Zamp Kelp

Visual Machines, Nagoya, Japan
Design for a trade fair stand for the German Design Exposition (with W Laubersheimer), 1989

Client: Rat für Formgebung, Frankfurt (Dr Michael Erlhoff)
Architect: Günter Zamp Kelp
Realisation: Wolfgang Laubersheim

Neanderthal Museum
Mettmann, 1994-1996

Client: Stiftung Neanderthal Museum
Sponsors: Nordrhein-Westfalen Stiftung and RWE
Architect: Günter Zamp Kelp and J Krauss / A Brandlhuber
Contractor: Hochtief AG, Düsseldorf

Expanding Space
Completion of an existing group of buildings, Meinerzhagen, 1992

Client: Einrichtungshaus Kessler, Meinerzhagen
Architect: Günter Zamp Kelp with Christoph Kessler

Green Glass Surface
Design of the entrance area of E Plus Mobilfunk Headquarters, Düsseldorf, 1995-96

Client: Josef Esch - Projekt GmbH
Architect: Günter Zamp Kelp
Contractor: Hochtief AG, Düsseldorf

Zero-Gravity Space
Alteratin of an Aldo van Eyck Building, Düsseldorf 1998 - 1999.

Client: Monika und Ulrike Schmela
Architect: Günter Zamp Kelp
Contractor: Bau- und Stuckunternehmen Swertz

Collaborators and Employees 1987-99
Cornelia Amtenbrink
Astrid Becker
Mark Braun
Roland Brieke
Tobias Bronner
Barbara Bruder
Volker Busse
Marcus Emde
Andreas Geitner
Oliver Gerlach
Marco Glashagen
Thomas Gutt
Andreas Hanke
Jörg Hundertpfund
Martin Jürgenliemk
Daniel Kas
Christoph Kessler
Alexei Kouzmine
Julius Krauss
Götz Leimkühler
Beate Mack
Andreas Marchel
Carlos Martin-Gonzales
Thomas Mitterer-Kuhn
Christoph Mörkl
Markus Reimann
Gregorz Ribatzky
Diego Rodriguez
Marie Celine Schäfer
Susanne Scheidler
Thomas Schüler
Martin Schulte-Frohlinde
Wolfgang Stockmeier
Karlheinz Winkens
Frank Wittmer

BIOGRAPHY

1941	Born in Bistritz, Romania
1944	Moves to Austria with his family
1959-67	Studies Architecture at the Technische Universität, Vienna. Awarded diploma
1967-69	Assistant Professor to Professor Karl Schwanzer, Institute for Design and Building Studies, Technische Universität, Vienna
1967	Founding Member of the group of artists and architects Haus-Rucker-Co in Vienna
1970	Studio in Düsseldorf
1971-72	Studio in New York Member of the Architektenkammer Nordrhein-Westfalen
1979	Awarded Kunstpreis Berlin (Fine Arts Award)
1981-82	Visiting Professor at Cornell University, USA, and Hochschule der Künste, Berlin
1987	Member of the Architektenkammer, Berlin
1988	Visiting Professor at the Städelsche Kunstschule, Division of Architecture University Professor at the Hochschule der Künste, Berlin, Faculty of Architecture, Building Design and Space Planning
1993	Head of Building Design and Space Planning and Communications Technology at the Hochschule der Künste, Berlin
1995	Awarded Gustav Meyer Preis der Stadt, Berlin
1996	Visiting Professor at the Technische Universität, Vienna
1998	Member of the Institut für Metropole, Architektur, Design
	Lives and works in Berlin and Düsseldorf

BIBLIOGRAPHY

Own Writings in Magazines / Newspapers:
'Dynamik der Leere', in *Kunstzeitschrift*, March 1985
'Architektur und Medialität', in *Daidalos*, No 35, March 1990
'Monument oder Ereignis', in *Daidalos*, No 40, June 1991
'Vom Monument zum Ereignis', in *Kunst als Revolte*, ed. K.Wilhelm, anabas Verlag, 1996
'Vom Hunger auf die Ursuppe', in *Die Welt*, 18 December 1998
'Vom Steinbruch zur Kulturdomäne', in *Architektur Bauforum*, no 6, 1997

Own Writings in Books / Catalogues:
'Am Tisch des 20 Jahrhunderts – Zukunftsperspektiven in Architektur und Stadtentwicklung' in L Burckhardt, *Design der Zukunft* Dumont Verlag, Cologne, 1982
'Die Haut als Botschaft' in *Formalhaut*, Verlag der Georg Buechner Buchhandlung, Darmstadt, 1988
'Die Frankfurter Medien Kaaba' in *Medien Kaaba, Projekte der Städelschule Frankfurt*, Verlag Jürgen Häuser, Darmstadt, 1990
'Die Steine selbst, so schwer sie sind' in TH Spiegelhalter, *Mediatecturen und Deponiekörper*, Häuser Verlag Darmstadt, 1992
'Bollwerk und Temporarium' in *Kunst im Bau, Schriftenreihe Forum / Band 1*, Bundes Kunst-und Ausstellungshalle, Bonn
'Stadtplatz und das zusätzliche Element' in *Projekt Platzgestaltung. Band 4*, Edition Deutsche Bank Bau Spar AG, Bauen und Wohnen, Coppenrath Verlag, Munich, 1996
Neanderthal Museum, exhibition catalogue, Galerie Aedes, Berlin, 1996
Mediale Aureolen für die Stadt. Zamp Kelp Projekte von 1987 – 1996, exhibition catalogue, Galerie Aedes, Berlin, 1996
Architektur und Medialität. ed. Heinrich Klotz, ZKM, Karlsruhe, 1990

PHOTO CREDITS p2 Michael Reisch; p6 Michael Pilz; p7 Gert Winkler; p8 Gert Winkler; p10 Gert Winkler, Archiv Haus-Rucker-Co; p12 Brigitte Hellgoth; p13 Archiv Haus-Rucker-Co; p14 Archiv Zamp Kelp; p15-16 Torsten Schmiedeknecht, Archiv Zamp Kelp; p17 Archiv Zamp Kelp; p18-20 Archiv Zamp Kelp; p20/21 (background image) Michael Reisch; p23 Julie Cook (image of Paul Davies); Archigram Archives; Paul Davies; p24 Julie Cook, Archiv HRC; p26 Paul Davies; p27 Julie Cook; p28/29 (background image) Archiv Zamp Kelp; p30-31 Archiv Zamp Kelp; p32-39 Archiv Zamp Kelp; p41-43 Susanne Jacoby; p44 Gerald Zugmann; p45-46 Christoph Reinhold; p48-51 Archiv Zamp Kelp; p52-53 Michael Reisch; p54 Archiv Zamp Kelp; p55 Archiv Zamp Kelp, Michael Reisch; p56 Archiv Zamp Kelp; p57 Michael Reisch; p58-64 Archiv Zamp Kelp; p65 Patrik Zier; p66-72 : Michael Reisch; p73: Laubner-Luftbild; p74-94 Archiv Zamp Kelp; p96-97 Michael Reisch; p98 Tomas Riehle p99 Archiv Zamp Kelp; p100–102 Tomas Riehle; p106 Torsten Schmiedeknecht, Julia Chance; p107 Susanne Jacoby, Torsten Schmiedeknecht; p108 Archiv Zamp Kelp; p110 Torsten Schmiedeknecht, Archigram Archives; p111 Horst Schmiedeknecht; p112 Archiv Zamp Kelp; p113 Photodisc; p114-115 Torsten Schmiedeknecht; p116 Archiv Haus-Rucker-Co; p117 Archiv Zamp Kelp; p118 Patrik Zier, Archiv Zamp Kelp; p119 Torsten Schmiedeknecht, Archiv Haus-Rucker-Co; p120 Archiv Haus-Rucker-Co; p120/121 (background) Michael Reisch; p122 Archiv Zamp Kelp; p123-125 Archiv Zamp Kelp

All translations from German by Torsten Schmiedeknecht except where stated.